Shipwrecks and Storm Clouds

Jim P Wright

Prodigal Press, Nashville, TN

Shipwrecks and Storm Clouds by Jim Wright

Published by: Prodigal Press, Nashville, Tennessee

Interior Design by: Thoughtful Revolution of Austin, Texas
Cover Design by: Thoughtful Revolution of Austin, Texas
Cover art by: Ryan Moon, ryanmoondesign.com
Editing by: Allison Vesterfelt

ISBN: 978-0-9897020-1-0

10 9 8 7 6 5 4 3 2 1

First Edition

"In discovering why we were created and what we were created for, it comes down to us having the beauty of spirit which glorifies our Creator. Jim has written about his life in such a way that none of us can walk away without being motivated to let go and let God! Jim is God's craftsmanship, His masterpiece! His story makes each one of us realize that if we take our place as part of the mosaic which creates His community, we are a life-giving community. I know that this book will carry the fragrance of Heaven."
Stephanie Fast // International speaker/ Destiny Ministries

"Wow! This autobiography of a well-known Pastor is a real page-turner as Jim Wright bares his life for all to see. This book speaks of God's relentless grace in running down a lost soul! Read this well-written book from Jim's heart and you will sense God's presence in every shipwreck and storm cloud life has."
Dr. Dan Tomlinson // Author of ``Birth Pangs``, ``A Woman's Silent Testimony`` and ``On the Road to Emmaus``

"If there was ever a wonder on how far God's love and grace can go to rescue someone, Pastor Jim's life journey will set at ease the question. This is a fascinating story that brings encouragement and hope to anyone who finds themselves at the end of their rope. Let this be a message from God to you and then pass it on to someone else who needs encouragement."
Perry A. Atkinson // President/General Manager, The Dove Radio & Television

Contents:

This book is dedicated to my loving, spirited, red headed, Irish wife Maureen, who for 25 years has loved me, stood by me, and accompanied me on countless trips to the ER.

To my son Tyler, who has become an incredible leader, writer, musician, artist, husband and daddy, in spite of my fathering techniques.

To my mother, who taught me, provided for me, guided me and released me. There will never be another hero like you.

To my faithful brother Mike who ran me over with his Baja buggy…twice!

To my two beautiful grandsons Liam and Quinn, who are the heartbeat and laughter of my life.

Thank you to Courtney Coker, for your countless hours spent editing my English iniquities. On a personal note, can I adopt you?

Prologue: Finding True North

Have you ever been lost?

Maybe, like me, you feel like you were born lost and spent much of your life just trying to figure out where you were going and how to get there.

Much of our existence is spent trying to identify our purpose in this life. We wander, often times aimlessly, for some direction, some harbor of reason.

The years of searching make us weary and we numb our hopelessness with self-abuse that buries our pain, along with our dignity and self respect.

The searching never ends and can, for many, last a lifetime.

Every human has great purpose and great potential. There is a beautiful and satisfying reason for our existence that far transcends money, careers or relationships.

Man is on a quest to find this purpose, He is searching, desperately on the hunt to capture it. And once he finds it, he sets his course and locks in.

This is man's true north.

Chapter 1: Father Issues

I didn't need a Father, didn't want a Father and certainly wasn't going to submit my life to another "Father". As far as I knew, fathers abandoned their children at a very young age and never kept their promises. Fathers allowed you to come visit them once a year and would take you to Disneyland and buy you a BB gun, but then they sent you home, only to be abused by another kind of father — a "step-father."

Step fathers were even worse than normal fathers. Step fathers would beat the tar out of you, your brother and your mom. Sometimes their violence was even delivered while still in their police uniform, complete with a gun and badge.

This was my experience with fathers. Needless to say, I had some real father issues and was unable to respect any authority. As far as I was concerned, cops and fathers were a bad joke and I was content to fight, snort, drink and smoke my foul memories away. I definitely didn't need another father in my life.

If God was a father, I wanted nothing to do with him.

My stepfather came into my life abruptly between the first and second grade, when my parents were divorced and my mother somehow ended up married to my dad's best friend. We lived in Santa Maria, California at the time until suddenly — seemingly overnight — my older brother Mike, my mom, my new step-dad and I were in a giant U-Haul, making our way up the I-5 corridor into the backcountry of Oregon.

My stepfather got a job as the one and only Sheriff of the small town of Williams and we all soon found out what a cruel and abusive man he was.

He began to lash out and hit my mom, right in front of my brother and I. As a second grader of only seven or eight years old, I was traumatized and began to cope by fighting at school and resorting to angry behavior. I must have signed the principal's paddle a hundred times in my career at Williams Elementary School.

After being punished at school, I would be punished again by my step dad at home with beatings and abusive language. I vowed that, one day, I would have revenge. But for the moment, all I could do was suppress my feelings and let the bitterness brew.

My mom, the complete antithesis of my step dad, was the kindest, most giving person on earth. She played piano in the little country church I was dragged to as a boy. We attended The Community Church in Williams, Oregon — it was there I first heard about some guy named Jesus and something about a cross on which this poor guy had to die.

I learned a lot of other things there, too. Ping-Pong was fun and could be played in the fellowship hall when adults were not around. Potlucks were good eats if you stayed away from Estelle's pickled green bean salad and mom's baked beans. Estelle's beans were awful and you didn't dare put any on your plate 'cuz, then, one way or another it would have to make it's way into your mouth and down your throat. Thems' was the rules! Mom's baked beans were good. However, anyone who consumed those little bombs would become dangerously gaseous.

My brother and I would laugh until we cried as all the old people in that little community church began to pass gas at those "pot lucks." The whole fellowship hall took on this geriatric, fermented bean odor. This chorus of harmonious flagellation was the only church choir we ever had and the only time the whole church was in "one accord". Whenever our Pastor would say from the pulpit, "God is in this place" I would think to myself, "you have to be kidding".

I saw my mom put money in a basket every week and thought about how much we needed that money. I needed a new pair of boots or jeans and more hooks for fishing — why the heck was mom giving this money away?! It was crazy. During the break between Sunday school and church, most of the deacons would have a cigarette out by the old tree in the front lawn. I never could figure out why we bothered with this church 'thing.' To me, it was a colossal waste of free time better spent fishing or hunting.

Most of these men knew the local Sheriff, my step dad, and thought he was a great guy. I was too afraid to tell anyone what an abusive, violent and cruel man he was. I figured that if I spoke up, nobody would believe me anyway — it wasn't worth the beating at home. There was no point. My mom and brother lived in this same world of fear.

As soon as I was old enough to ditch the church scene, I did.

Being abandoned at a young age by my father and suffering abuse at the hand of my step dad caused huge issues in my life which lasted long after the abuse ended. An ever-present feeling of rejection and worthlessness plagued me for years and shaped every aspect of my life. I looked at the world through the lens of self-doubt, yet longed for acceptance through any means possible.

My perceived lack of worth dominated my psyche and my efforts to achieve value in the eyes of others was a relentless, misguided pursuit. Everyday, in everything I did, I longed to be loved and accepted.

As I became a man, I tried to shake off these feelings, but I can see now how I was *always* trying to find my identity, to resolve this question: who was I besides a rejected and unwanted kid? Without the love and guidance from a father I was on my own to find out who I was. *Was I an athlete? Was I a good student? Was I funny or smart or kind? Who was I?*

As a really young kid, I was angry. Though I could not identify it at the time, I was hurt and afraid, and I dealt with these feelings by fighting and acting out in class. Fighting became 'the norm' for me in elementary school. Unleashing my anger on any boy who dared to provoke me was how I dealt with the abuse of my stepfather. I didn't see the connection then, but now as I look back I can see it very clearly.

I recognized the injustice of my stepfather and the cruel way he treated my mom, my brother and myself. But since I was unable to oppose this injustice at home, I held it in until I was on the playground at school. It was there my rage expressed itself. During these years, at Williams Elementary School, I became used to drawing blood — literal, physical blood of those around me. The cycle of violence had begun at home and I was acting out the very thing I hated: abuse.

I rebelled against any authority in my life. My bus driver gave me a citation one afternoon on the 2-mile trip from the school to my home. When I disembarked, I went directly to our chicken coop, collected about 2 dozen eggs, climbed high into a nearby Ponderosa Pine with ammunition in tow and waited for the bus to return down the road. When the bus came into view, I unleashed all the eggs onto the bus. I failed to consider the fact that the driver might stop, but she did, and there I was, totally exposed in the upper branches of the tree.

Later that evening I was visited by a local deputy and cited for "recklessly endangering others". Another brutal beating by my stepfather followed this event.

Later I tended to my wounds in my tree fort, the place I called "my home away from home" for many years.

I know my story is not unique. The details might be different, but the themes are the same. People get hurt and become afraid. They have a compromised identity, which makes them feel empty. They subsequently act out in rage, self-abuse, substance abuse or are overtaken by an insatiable desire for material things.

As someone who has walked down many of these paths, hoping to recover my identity, let me speak with authority and conviction: those roads are never-ending and lead to nowhere. There is never a destination, only rest stops spread at great distances along the way. These roads, which I feverishly sped down, were all I knew. By the time I left my twenties, I was tired of traveling this journey.

Life had no purpose, no direction and no hope. Living itself had become mundane. Days passed into months, and months into years of the unanswered questions: *Who am I? Can I ever be happy? Can I ever be rid of this hate and guilt in my life? Can I ever have a fresh start?* The worst part was, I was constantly battling empty and lonely feelings in the depths of my heart.

There had to be something more to life than just existing — right?

My young heart became hard. Reckless decisions began to rule me. I would need a huge break for any change to ever take place in my life.

Chapter 2: Alone

I felt alone my entire life. Even though I was surrounded by people, I had this constant sense I was invisible. I felt there was nothing of value in me. Even though I was quite extroverted, inside I felt alone and hopeless to change my circumstances.

Our little farm on Kincaid Road in Williams, Oregon consisted of a cow or two (depending on the day) a few goats, sheep, pigs, chickens, rabbits, dogs and an occasional injured raccoon or bird. All of our animals, with the exception of the dogs, were raised for food; and all slaughtering, cleaning and packaging of the meat was done on the farm. Naturally, I learned to kill and skin animals as a young boy and also managed to tend to a large vegetable garden.

I was in the fourth grade when I was first introduced to a local livestock club called 4H. It was a club for kids which taught us to use our head, heart, hands and health to better our community and ourselves. We practiced these principles by raising animals throughout the year and we eventually brought them to the county fair in the summer to be judged for showmanship.

We would present our animals for ribbons and then sell them at auction for the slaughterhouse, which in retrospect seems kind of morbid (selling our pets for human consumption) but that is how it all worked. We would try not to get too attached to our animals, but it was always a tearful farewell when "Ethel" or

"Buster" or any of our pets were taken away to the knife.

We were a poor family and I got into 4H by accident. Each year, our local community had a "Pioneer Roundup" at the big corral on Davidson road. It was a time when all the locals got together and drank beer, looked at cowgirls, barrel raced, log rolled, speed cut logs with chainsaws and two-man bow saws, threw axes, climbed poles and looked at cowgirls (oh, did I mention that already?).

Williams was a real redneck community — along with the local hippies who my friends and I would spy on while they skinny-dipped in Williams creek (very hairy people). Anyway, it was at this "Pioneer Roundup," called the Gymkhana, where I received my first 4H animal.

I was entered into a pie-eating contest where each of us kids would line up and eat pie without using our hands. All the local women would bake blackberry pie and place one in front of each contestant and, at the whistle, we would each plow our face into the pie and begin to inhale. The first one to swallow it *all* won a ribbon.

Now, the ribbons weren't much more than a piece of polyester to pin on, but they meant *everything* to kids who had nothing. If you had a ribbon, you wore it proudly and were esteemed highly in the hierarchy of local rednecks. For me, a ribbon represented personal value. If I could somehow obtain a ribbon, I could wear it so everybody could see I was not invisible, I had worth.

I ate pie, but when the contest was over, I had no ribbon. I tried my luck at other events, such as barrel racing on my neighbors Shetland pony, throwing the axe, and few others, each time with no ribbon.

I *had* to win something. It meant everything to me.

There was an event coming up on the last day called the "greased pig" contest, where a 40 to 50 lb. piglet would be completely smeared with bearing grease some logger had in the back of his truck and released into the arena. The contestants would all stand behind a line while the spectators lined up on the top rail of the arena fence. On the whistle, we would all charge for the pig to catch it.

I was "all in" on this one. I wasn't just going to wear a ribbon; I was going to take home a pig.

So when the whistle blew, we all charged for the innocent little sausage, and Porky ran like the wind. Kids were falling and flying and running into each other. It was a bloody affair. Just when I thought Jay or Cliff or one of my other friends had it, it would slip out of their grasp and continue its terrified escape to nowhere. It turned right, toward me, squealed and threatened to run right over the top of me. This was my time — I was made for this!

I lunged onto the little squealing piece of bacon and hung on for dear life. Sure enough, Porky collapsed in exhaustion and I brought home the pig that afternoon.

He had to line our freezer a little earlier than we expected, due to injuries he received in the mayhem. I was heartbroken. So my sweet mother talked with some local farmers and acquired another piglet for me to raise for 4H.

It was an unorthodox way of getting into the 4H club, but I was in, and I had a story to tell. I was the guy who caught the greased pig at the "Pioneer Roundup". I was famous; a Redneck celebrity. I had value.

When the County Fair finally rolled around that summer, I had a full-sized pig to enter and got a ribbon for showmanship, which I proudly displayed on the wall of my room. I was the only one who ever saw it, but it meant everything to me.

My pig was sold to the market and I walked away with some money in my pocket to buy another one the following year.

Fair was a huge part of life for those of us growing up in Williams. It was the highlight of our year as kids. I had a sense of belonging and felt a little less alone knowing our town was united by this event.

Josephine County Fairgrounds in Grants Pass had dorms for 4H participants so we didn't have to travel the 25 miles home each night only to get back early the next morning in order to care for our animals. We had "Barn Duty" every day and had to feed, water, change straw, sweep and keep the pig area of the barn clean for all the city folk who came to see what a pig looked like.

When we were not on "Barn Duty" we would wander down to the carnival and enjoy the exciting atmosphere created by the rides, contests and strangely pierced and inked Carny's who worked there. We never had the money to participate in anything big, but there was one event I tried my hand at. It was the dime toss.

There were hundreds of glass saucers, plates and bowls stacked inside a tent waiting for carnival-goers to throw dimes in an attempt to land one inside of a glass for a prize. I won a few glass bowls I was sure my mom would love and then got an idea: there were hundreds of dollars worth of dimes on the floor of the tent that were apparently left untouched until the fair was over.

Each day there was more and more money sitting on the floor of the tent. I talked with my friends, Jay and Cliff, who were sleeping in my same dorm, and we decided it would be an easy robbery. All we had to do was get up at about 3:00am and go down to the dime toss. We would get under the tent wall and load up on the booty.

We figured it was an easy way to make big money. So we did it.

The Carnival shut down at 1:00am and we readied our assault around 3:00am. We slipped under the tent, filled our front and back pockets (and even the pouches created by the inverted bellies of our shirts). Then we made our exit and ran back to the dorms where we unloaded our prize in our sleeping bags.

We did it! It was the greatest heist in human history and we were rich!

We kept it quiet (as brilliant thieves would). Then, the next afternoon after barn duty, we made our way back down to the carnival area to spend our loot. First things first, we got ourselves a hamburger, fries and a coke at one of the concessions. Then we purchased some ride tickets for "the Hammer". Drunk with our riches, we didn't think this completely through, and paid for everything in dimes.

We were not the sharpest tools in the shed — not by a long shot.

So, there we were, in line, getting our burgers (the total was around $5.50) and I reach in and pull out 55 dimes. Jay and Cliff did the same. We ate and laughed and then got in line for carnival ride tickets. Same routine. $20 worth of tickets, 200 dimes. We were crying with laughter, spinning upside down in the "Hammer" when, over the loud speaker, we heard: "Jim Wright, Cliff Thomason, Jay Carnes, please report to the main office".

Busted.

I know, right?

I was sick. Our plan failed. I was going to be somebody's boyfriend in prison. We made our way to the office, where we were interrogated by the police. They made a juvenile arrest and turned us over to our parents. My stepdad was the one who came to get me and he showed up in his police uniform. That night, I received the beating of my life, with bruises on my body that lasted for weeks.

This is how I ended up at New Hope Christian School. Odd how Christian schools are often viewed as the fix for hurting children, don't you think? My parents would soon find no program, Christian school or church camp would be the solution to my rebellious or criminal ways.

Nevertheless, I began the following September, stepping in as a 5th grader at New Hope Christian school while all my friends went off to Murphy Elementary or Lincoln Savage Middle School. I was devastated. I wasn't a Christian! What was I doing in a Christian School?

My friends got to start playing tackle football but New Hope had no such sports program. I had to ride the school bus each day to Lincoln Savage and watch all my friends get off and go to school. Then I would stay on the bus and ride the next few miles to New Hope. Or, as my friends would laughingly call it, "No Hope".

It was a rough four years. I was in and out of trouble and barely passed my classes. My summers were spent bucking hay, changing sprinkler pipe, fishing the local creeks and ponds and tending animals for 4H.

As if there wasn't enough trauma in my life, one summer afternoon, just before my 7th grade year, my stepfather rolled up to the house in a big moving truck while my mom was at work. He had some gal with him who waited in the truck. I later found out this was his girlfriend.

He ordered my brother and I to help him load up the truck with his dozens of guns, reloading equipment, and various other valuables. Then he drove away and I never saw him again. When my mom arrived home from work, it was my brother Mike and

I who had to break the news. I was so glad he was gone, but on the other hand, I was now *sure* fathers were losers. I continued to scramble for identity and manhood without any direction. Where was I to turn?

The lessons I learned in those childhood years were as follows:

- Life was a big screwed up mess.
- Fathers were a joke. They were uncommitted, violent and temporary.
- 4H was fun, but culminated in the death of your pet.
- If you were a bad kid, you had to go to Christian School.
- Drugs and alcohol were a great escape — like medication to numb the pain of life.

I would later find out that, although I felt alone in this "school of life" I had unwillingly been enrolled in, the majority of kids in our culture were enrolled in the same school. The lessons were the same: Brokenness, abandonment, and abuse. It wasn't just me. We were all filled with hatred and bitterness. It was epidemic. Was there a way out?

Chapter 3: Oceans of Pain

Some pain cuts so deep it seems impossible to ever recover. Some pain is inflicted by adults in our childhood, but we will never forget. This story is one of those wounds.

Behind our home lay a pond, a field and an endless forest. This was our backyard playground. The forest gave us ample opportunity to make tree forts, hide contraband, and explore to our heart's content. It was here we cut all of our firewood for winter. It was here we played "Cowboys and Indians" with *real* BB guns.

As we grew older, the guns became larger. We shot every living creature we could put in our sights — but never our farm animals. To tell the truth, I am pretty sure I shot the cows a few times, mostly the neighbors' cows, but only with a BB gun. My brother and I would shoot blue jays, crows, lizards, skunks, and of course, the grey squirrels (which we would later eat).

One day, my stepfather told us he had lost his wallet in the woods and would give us a reward if we could find it and return it. A few weeks later, my brother and I were running back from the forest and through the field when I saw a black object in the tall grass. I backtracked to see what it was...it was a wallet.

I opened it and saw it was, in fact, my step-dad's. I was so thrilled I had found it. He would be so proud of me. This was the reward I was looking for! For once, my stepdad would be proud of me instead of telling me what he normally told me — that I was an idiot. I can still hear those words coming out of his mouth like it was yesterday.

I ran as fast as my little feet would carry me and ran right onto the back porch, yelling I had found his wallet. He came out of the house, took the wallet in his hands, checked its contents and then proceeded to accuse me of stealing it. The only reason I brought it back, he said, was because of the reward I had been promised. He said he knew that if he promised a reward I would get greedy and return it.

I protested. I had *not* stolen the wallet but had found it in the field. He called me a liar and proceeded to pull the buggy whip out of the corner of the porch and made me bend over the chest freezer sitting in the corner. He beat me and laid stripes on me that lasted for weeks.

I hated him. I grew harder and harder and became more and more hateful toward everybody. Life was unfair and I was going to get out of Williams at the first opportunity.

I thought of running away several times but I knew that if I ever got caught, he would beat me so badly I would never walk again. Besides, I had no place to go and I loved my mom and my brother. So I stayed and continued to live in fear.

It was a regular event in our home that my step dad would beat my mother and throw her around the house. My brother and I lived in the attic that had been converted into bedrooms. Vents had been installed to allow the heat to get upstairs from the wood stove in the living room. One vent came up from my mom and stepdad's bedroom downstairs, so I would listen through the opening, hearing him tell her terrible things and call her terrible names. He would hit her and choke her. As an 11-year-old boy, I didn't know what to do.

I thought, so many times of loading my .22 rifle with the 18 rounds it held and going downstairs to unload it on him. I was forced to think of killing a man at 11 years old. No child should ever have to be in the middle of that kind of mess.

At one point in my stepfather's career as the local sheriff, he was assigned a K9 partner. The K9s name was "Hard" and he was a pure German Shepherd, trained in German commands. It was always fun to have a new animal around the house and my brother and I soon befriended Hard.

My stepdad used us boys to help keep the K9 sharp with his attack skills. He would make me put on a big "padded arm", which I could barely hold. Then, from a hundred feet away, I would call out a German command to have the dog attack me. I was instructed to let the dog take me to the ground and hold still so he wouldn't bite me.

I remember seeing this huge dog running right at me and baring his teeth. My job was *not to flinch*, to allow him to attack. I had to be sure to hold out the padded arm so he would bite into it and not my legs or face or other arm. I was terrified and told my stepdad so, but the K9 attack practice continued.

One day, after being released from Williams Elementary School and getting off the school bus at our home on Kincaid road, I experienced another trauma that haunted me for years. It was my routine to go inside the house, head to my room, change clothes and go to the tree house where I spent most of my free time.

As I came around to the back of the house, I heard a strange sound coming from behind the woodshed out by the pump house. I looked around the corner and saw my 4H pig on the ground, tangled in a chain, with Hard eating out its entrails. Hard had broken his chain and attacked my pig. I couldn't believe what I was seeing. This was the pet pig I had purchased with my own money. Now my stepdad's dog had killed it and was chewing on it.

I screamed and cried as I took in this painful sight.

Hard had blood all over him and would growl if I advanced.

I called my mom at work (which was for emergencies only) and she called a local farmer friend who came over and got the dog and pig separated. Frank (my stepdad) had been notified and pulled in to the driveway in his police cruiser. He talked things over with the local farmer friend and the man left, only to return minutes later with a handful of sharp knives. He began to butcher out the pig for the meat.

I was told to help the man and I knew what would happen if I didn't obey. So there I was, hands bloody, helping butcher out my pet pig. It was traumatic enough to sell a pig to auction at the end of the year. But to get it's blood on my own hands was too much for my young heart.

My heart became even harder that day as we packaged up the meat and put it in our freezer. I would be forced to eat this meat at dinnertime. I had to eat my own pet.

Authority was modeled as careless and ruthless. I learned, by example, that authority did what it wanted, when it wanted and how it wanted without any concern for others. It felt like slavery to me. I had no voice. Any effort to express feelings about a given issue was answered by a slap across the face.

I was being shaped by the fathers in my life and becoming more and more entrenched in hatred and bitterness. These things would play a huge role in my marriage and family in the future. I had no idea the man I was going to become but began to catch glimpses of how I was being shaped by my careless living.

I swore to myself so many times that I would never be like my stepfather or my real father. I would never abandon my family, if I ever had one. The irony of this is that the more I held on to the bitterness and hatred, the more I saw myself becoming just like them. This realization infuriated me even further and deepened the emotional dysfunction taking place in my heart.

I was bitter and hated my stepfather who was bitter and a hater.

Was I going to be just another link in the chain of dysfunction that traced back generations? Was it possible I could be the one link to break the ongoing cycle of hatred and bitterness? It seemed I was trapped, destined to simply strengthen the chain. How could I be fixed? Was I going to need years of therapy and antidepressants? Perhaps I could just self-medicate through drugs and alcohol. I didn't know the answers, but I definitely knew I was broken.

The extent of my brokenness would manifest itself in the next decade of life. I would finally realize I was so shattered that no recovery seemed possible.

I was too broken to be fixed. Or so I thought, anyway.

Chapter 4: Escape

I was thirteen years old when my stepfather ran off with his girlfriend. Mom took up the mantle of raising us boys alone, and she worked hard. She would rise early, before the sun came up, and pack us lunches for school. Then she would drive the 25 miles, on icy winter roads, to work her shift as a checker at Safeway in Grants Pass. She would always make us breakfast, read us our morning devotions and write down instructions for our chores when we got home from school.

Her schedule was always posted on the "reefer" (refrigerator) so we knew when she would be home for the night. Sometimes she would work the late shift and wouldn't be home until midnight. But the following mornings, she was always up early for our morning routine.

My mom is one of those rare women who fought for her kids and poured the Word into us every day until we left home. She is a true hero.

Despite my mother's dedication, at that point in my life I was *not* interested in spiritual things. My father(s) had abandoned my brother and I and hurt my mom; a heavenly father did not interest me. I was angry, hurt and confused.

It was during this time of life I began to sneak over to my neighbor's shed and steal Boones Ferry wine to get drunk. It was hilarious, I thought. I would steal a bottle and go out to the "tree fort" my brother and I had constructed in an old oak tree in the woods and drink the whole bottle. I would talk with myself and have long conversations with my imaginary dad, telling him what was on my mind.

Other times I would just read the girly magazines I had stashed. I'm not going to lie, I would mostly just look at the pictures — very educational. This is how I learned about sex. It wasn't exactly the best education, but it was an education nevertheless.

It wasn't long after I started drinking I also began smoking weed. All my friends at this point had, unlike Bill Clinton, begun inhaling. Weed was easily available and about half of the 2000 person population in my hometown grew their own. In fact, most of the weed grown in Williams was ranked among the best in the nation. I soon learned "gardening" could be very profitable.

I would start my plants from seeds I had purchased from friends at school, then transplant them into our family garden under the disguise of tomato plants. It was my job to weed the garden on Saturdays, so I would have a whole row of marijuana plants growing — right next to Kincaid road. When they got about a foot high, I transplanted them to the woods, not far from a creek, and tended them until they were usable.

This became a lifestyle for me throughout high school. I got busted a few times over the years at Hidden Valley High School. One time my mom found a couple pounds of weed in my backpack. Another time I was caught red-handed in the school parking lot, smoking a joint with a friend in my VW Baja Bug. I went to drug school and had to watch movies of bad car accidents that warned the viewer how bad smoking pot was. I could've cared less. I was going to smoke pot, sell it to make gas money and buy food at the cafeteria at school.

It wasn't long after I started high school I began eating mushrooms and dropping acid. My heart hurt. I was angry and confused — drugs made me forget the pain and mask the sickness in my head and heart.

Pain requires attention. It cannot be ignored. It must be addressed one way or another. Have you ever considered that? We all have pain, and we *all* have found the medication to best cover it up. Temporary as it may be, this numbing agent is what we will gravitate towards. The only remedy I could find to numb the pain in my heart was drugs and alcohol.

To make matters worse, I was an unrestrained and violent person when I used drugs. I was wild and crazy and would strike at anybody. I became known as a fighter and would get into a brawl at just about every party I attended.

One time I threw a cue ball through the back windshield of a truck while my friends and I were cruising up and down 6th and 7th street in Grants Pass. The three guys in the truck in front of us had flipped us off and, for some reason, the 56 Chevy Bel Air Coupe my friend Rick was driving had a cue ball rolling around on the floor boards. I grabbed the ball, hung myself out the window far enough to get a good throwing position, and launched the ball perfectly into the back window of the flipper's truck, shattering it.

They pulled over and so did we. The fight put one of them in the hospital.

We were picked up later by the Josephine County cops and arrested. This became routine for me for the next several years; I was always in and out of trouble with the law for fighting and drinking. Staying high as much as possible had become my new normal. Ten years went by, years during which I was either drunk or high every single day. I carried Visine in my pocket to clear my red eyes and learned to be what is known as a "functioning user".

It felt good to be high and, more importantly, it allowed me the opportunity to escape reality.

My older brother Mike was a straight-A student and everybody loved him. He was a great athlete and captain of the basketball team at New Hope Christian School. He was Valedictorian of his class and went to college right out of high school. Mike pursued his talents as an artist and became an art teacher. He was a Christian and did the right things and made the right decisions.

I, on the other hand, flunked my classes, had no vision for the future and lived in the moment. I had lost hope at a young age. Without hope, we become wanderers, flowing along in whatever current we find ourselves in. Hopelessness is a terrible state to live in. The despair that lingers in this place is real — it's dark and it's deadly.

At first, the numbing effect of drugs and alcohol were good enough. The problem was: drugs and alcohol never addressed the problem, they only numbed the symptoms. One day I *would* have to address the root of the problem in my heart, but the longer I went on like I was, the further I walked down the road of bitterness and regret, the more difficult it would become to address the initial wound.

Maybe you can relate. Maybe you feel hurt or angry, but you don't even know why anymore. Maybe you've been walking down a similar road but you haven't considered how you got on this road in the first place. Maybe you're asking yourself the questions I was asking myself back then: *Will I ever have hope? Will I ever have purpose? Will tomorrow always be filled with trouble and hate?*

Chapter 5: Broken Glass

It was 1980, the year which held an unforgettable Memorial Day weekend. As a sophomore at Hidden Valley High School, I was playing right field on a softball team and we had just finished a game. It was a warm afternoon and a perfect time to go flirt with the girls at the festivities at Riverside Park. My friend Mike and I jumped into his grandfather's old International pickup truck and Mike took the wheel.

We rolled down the windows and reveled in the victory we had just experienced on the field. The music was cranked up. We laughed. We savored the moment. Our friends Nick and Rick were also part of the team and were a few minutes in front of us. We thought for sure we could catch up to them.

We quickly did, coming right up on their bumper as we raced down New Hope road. We were only about seven or eight miles from town when we began bearing down on them, waiting impatiently for the right opportunity to pass. We knew a long straightaway was coming and, when it did, we made our move.

We had just pulled out to pass them near Fish Hatchery Road when everything went terribly wrong. I am still not quite sure how it went south so fast, but it did. In the process of passing, Nick's car swerved toward us. Mike braked hard and we pulled to the right really quickly, barely missing them. Mike corrected the truck back to the left, but turned way too hard and we crossed back into the road. That's when I heard the noise.

That noise was so loud and violent and traumatic. I had bad dreams with that same noise for months following the accident.

We flew across the road in that old truck, launched off the edge of the ten-foot irrigation ditch and hit the embankment on the other side. The first impact threw me face-first through the windshield and slammed my head onto the hood; the truck continued to flip over several times and I was somehow thrown back through the glass into the truck cab again as it settled upside down in the ditch.

I couldn't see and my eyes felt like someone had thrown gravel in them. I later discovered it was glass. I felt around, completely disoriented, trying to find the handle to the door. We were upside down and all I could do was feel my way out of the truck. I found a place where I could squeeze out of the windshield. Then, as soon as I got out of the truck, I began to run away.

I was so tired of pain. I was so sick of being hurt. I just wanted to get away from it. My home life had been painful. The beatings I had regularly received at the hands of my stepfather had been painful. I was so done with being hurt and just wanted to escape. In this case, I was literally trying to run away from the pain.

With blood all over me, I ran down the edge of the ditch. I began to regain a bit of my sight. Then I heard someone yell for me to lie down, and I did.

It was then I heard the scream. This was no ordinary scream; this was the type of scream that raised the hair on the back of your neck. It was the scream of major trauma. My friend Mike was struggling to get out of the truck after he discovered a major compound fracture in his left leg.

He was screaming.

He too, was lacerated and broken. We were both really 'jacked up'.

My 7th grade English teacher from New Hope Christian School, Mrs. Vannoy, lived right across the street from the accident and she called 911 to report the crash. Mike not only had a badly destroyed leg but also had his chest crushed and was having a hard time breathing. He survived but had to use a cane to walk for the rest of his life.

Our friends in the other vehicle had turned around at this point and Rick came to my aid. As soon as he looked at me, he turned his head and heaved. I knew I was really injured but it was hard to tell how badly. I remember putting my hands on my face and not recognizing what I was feeling. Things were in the wrong place and nothing felt right.

I was talking funny and my skin was slippery and felt like a deflated balloon. Something was wrong with my mouth and everything began to really hurt. The pain kept coming in waves as shock set in. The ambulance finally arrived and transported us — "code three" — to Josephine General Hospital.

My mom remembers hearing the ambulance as it went by Safeway where she was working at the time and praying to God her little Jimmy was not in that ambulance. It would be only minutes later she would get the call. I was the one in the ambulance.

I remember my sweet mother coming into the hospital room as the doctors were trying to stop my bleeding. She looked at me with eyes full of motherly love and voiced her affection. She cried and I could tell she didn't think I was going to live. I had lost a ton of blood and the doctors needed to get me into surgery right away.

I was in surgery for four hours as they braced and stitched my face back together.

I was in the hospital for several days. And after several hundred stitches and drainage tubes still in my face, I was released to go home. But the trauma of this accident was far from over.

As the weeks passed and I had my stitches removed, the injuries gave way to red, puffy scars all over my face. I had major marks around my eyes and nose; a patch of my head was shaved, leaving the gashes exposed. There were lines along my lower lip, chin and throat. The main scar ran through my right ear all the way down to the left side of my neck. I looked like Frankenstein.

I remember looking into the mirror and barely recognizing myself. I would stare at my reflection and think: *I will never have a girlfriend again. I am so ugly, worthless, angry, and bitter.*

Thoughts of suicide entered and left my mind. I had the means of ending it all right there in the house. We had guns and I knew how to use them.

I knew a time was coming soon where I would have to go back to school and face all of my friends and enemies. When you're 16 years old, you don't want to go to school even if you have a pimple on your face, let alone after you've been transformed into a freak. Even the thought of it was unbearable.

The day finally came. I remember going to my first class on my first day back to school. One of the girls in the class looked at me and said, out loud, "*Oh My God.*"

That was it. I left the class, got on the pay phone (we didn't have cell phones in 1980), called my mom and told her I wanted to come home. My mom is a wise woman and told me I needed to stay. I needed to stand up and get through this. She reassured me the scars would look better in time and I was going to have to get used to the funny looks and remarks.

I was angry and depressed. This was a turning point in life for me. I ramped up my substance abuse and absolute recklessness.

Life was hard, unjust, and a really sick joke. I was thoroughly wounded. My face would eventually heal, and the wounds would fade to scars. But the wounds in my heart, my psyche — they were showing no sign of healing at all.

How does one find healing in his heart after the seeds of bitterness have grown into a thriving garden of hatred? Is denial an option? Could I forget that my life had been so *weird*? Could I just put it all behind me and tuck it away into a place I would never find it?

Would I need decades of counseling and end up living my life on anti-depressants? The thought of that worsened my hopelessness and depression.

Was I seriously destined to become the very thing I despised? Was I going to live my life an angry and violent man, unable to hold a job due to my short fuse? Would I go through multiple divorces? *C'mon*, I wanted to ask, *was this my destiny, my purpose?*

I felt like I was quickly running out of choices.

If you are still reading, you have either pegged me as crazy and can't believe you are wasting time with this *or* you can't possibly stop reading because you know exactly how I was feeling. Perhaps you could have written those exact words.

Statistically, you're the latter.

Abuse forced upon a child creates a monster of rage. Some say the only hope in such cases is medication. Some say it is forgiveness. Some say there is no hope. At the time, I didn't know what to believe. I know differently now, but back then, I opted for medication of my own choosing.

Chapter 6: Two Captains

High school was *way* overrated, so I quit my senior year —just weeks before graduation. An opportunity came up for me to begin fishing commercially and, the way I saw it, this was an opportunity to get away from everyone and everything.

One of my friend's grandfathers owned and operated a fishing boat in Coos Bay, Oregon and I was offered a job as a deck hand. For me, this was like winning the lottery. No more school? No more memories of the violent home where I grew up? No more cops who knew me by name? I was going out to sea and would perhaps never return. For me, there was no choice.

Freedom was before me and I was going to grab hold of it. I was going to get out of Williams, be my own man and get to start all over. A fresh start was exactly what I needed.

I took the job and left everything behind.

It was almost euphoric. I could not believe my fortune.

But it didn't turn out exactly how I expected.

Weeks after I was offered the job I was out at sea, heading to Hawaii on the waters of the Pacific. I would fish for several years, on several boats, out of several ports. A few years into my life at sea, I became vividly aware that life at sea was more than just an exciting and dangerous job. It was also an environment that, given the right combination of volatile ingredients, was deadly.

I had been working for months on a dry-docked boat at Moss Landing Harbor, California. The 65-foot jig boat named "Two Captains" needed repairs and paint for its next voyage in the Midway fleet. So we geared it up for Albacore fishing — adding deck tanks for fuel to make the long journey to Hawaii where we would restock. From there, we would hunt for the Pacific mother load of Tuna.

The first boat I fished on out of Coos Bay, Oregon was the "Janita", the second was the "3 Jacks" and finally, as an experienced fish puller, I was making a higher percentage of the catch on the "Two Captains". Fishing alone with just the Captain meant a ton more work but also a lot more money. So I wasn't complaining.

We put out to sea and arrived in Honolulu 13 days after our departure from Moss Landing. Docking in Koala Basin, Honolulu, I reunited with other fishing buddies from different parts of the world. Some had fished in Japan the previous year and were returning to the Midway fleet; others came in from Alaska and various other landings on the West Coast.

Commercial fishing was a dangerous life on many fronts. It paid well and porting in Koala Basin in Honolulu was a nice perk, but we all carried guns while in port and watched our backs. "Howlies," or white people, were not welcome in certain parts of town so we had to be careful where we spent our money.

We had a great first trip, filling our hold with 44 tons of tuna and delivering it to Hawaiian Tuna Packers. The price for albacore tuna was high at the time and, as a kid who grew up in a poor home in Williams, Oregon, I had never seen so much cash. I bought whatever I wanted and blew through thousands of dollars in just a few days.

For the first time in my life, I could buy new stuff. The drinking age in Hawaii was 18 at the time, so I drank at all of the clubs my friends and I wanted to enter. Most of them were places my mother would definitely *not* approve of. But I was free. I was a man. And compared to the money I used to make bucking hay in Williams, I was rich.

We restocked, refueled and went back out to sea on our second trip that season. My Captain and I were not getting along too well, to say the least. I was a punk kid with a huge chip on his shoulder and my Captain was a drunk who started his day with a shot of Jack and continued nursing the bottle until he would eventually pass out. It was on this trip I, too, gave way to hard liquor. I added this habit to the serene state and euphoric high I was already experiencing from smoking Hawaiian buds. I am surprised neither one of us just fell overboard and got lost at sea.

We were catching a lot of fish, picking up a few hundred a day. There were times the fish would surface and frenzy. In these short bursts of feeding, I would throw several hundred fish on the boat in 30-40 minutes before they would dive back into the depths, allowing the calm to return.

It was a rush like no other. There would be fish flopping three feet deep along the deck with blood and squid everywhere. Often times the fish would blow half digested squid right in my face as I pulled them out of the water. It was awesome!

We were making money and on our way to having another full load when it happened.

Things had taken a turn for the worse in my relationship with the captain. I had no idea how to work through problems, ask for forgiveness, give forgiveness to others, or deal with anger. I had zero tools in my bag for any kind of healthy relationship. On the other hand, my captain would be so drunk I would often find him passed out in the captain's chair at the wheel. He was angry and bitter. I was arrogant and untamed — not a great combination.

We could never get more than 65 feet away from each other — bow to stern.

We had been at each other's throats for several weeks and I was determined to find another boat to fish on after this eight-week trip. Bitterness had taken root and I would spend my days in the cockpit of the stern, smoking weed while he drank his Jack in the wheelhouse. It was a disaster waiting to happen.

I will never forget the day it did.

We began our day with the usual smart-mouth remarks to each other, I made coffee and headed to the stern to put out the lines. If I ever needed help in the stern, I would pull a line to ring a bell and he would come to assist me. I rarely pulled the line. I would rather struggle through any problem than deal with him. But this particular day, while I was working the stern —mending line, sharpening hooks and pulling the occasional tuna, Paul (my captain) began to yell at me for something.

Honestly, I wasn't in the mood, so I flipped him off with some vulgar remark and turned back to my business. That's when I heard a familiar sound. It was the sound of the gaff hook being pulled out of the small, but deep, wooden box at the top of the cockpit.

The gaff hook was a baseball bat with a six-inch stainless hook on the end to land large fish or those lightly hooked. I used it when I felt the need to sink it into the head of a fish in order to get it onto the boat. I knew the sound. I had retrieved the gaff thousands of times. So as soon as I heard the sound, I looked back and saw Paul raise the gaff hook over his head. It all happened so fast, but I was able to get my arm up and my head down just as the stainless hook came in with a fierce, debilitating stroke.

He was going to kill me. He had lost his mind.

I reacted by launching out of the cockpit, grabbing him, and throwing him hard onto the deck, pinning him down with all of my 180 pounds. The gaff hook bounced out of his hands. I had control of him, but *now what*? I couldn't exactly call the cops. I couldn't get away. I was officially screwed.

My only option was to kill him, throw him over the side, wait a few hours as I would steer the boat away from him. Then I could get on the radio to announce I had woken up from a nap, only to find Paul was overboard. The story would be an easy sell because everyone knew he was a drunk —that is, everyone except his brother-in-law Dean, the captain of another boat in the fleet. I had heard Paul on the radio recently telling Dean I was a pain in the ass and he was going to look for another deck hand after this trip. Dean would be suspicious.

All of this went through my head as I pulled Paul from the deck. I decided to let him up, after delivering a few choice words accompanied by blows to his face. As I got off of him, I noticed the blood. In the scuffle, Paul had acquired a compound fracture. He had a bone coming through his upper chest and poking through his t-shirt. Blood was everywhere. He needed medical attention and we were 1000 miles at sea.

We calmed down, he sobered up quickly and apologized. How do you forgive somebody who just tried to kill you? I was having a little bit of trouble trusting him at this point. We had guns on the boat. I knew where he had one stashed in the wheelhouse but I didn't know if he had one in his quarters.

He got on the radio and called for assistance from anybody in the fleet who might have a doctor or nurse on board —anyone who could come set his collar bone and stitch him up. I stood behind him with the gaff hook in hand just in case he began to announce he had been attacked by his deckhand, or some partial truth that would stir up a threat against my life.

A few hours later, another boat from the fleet arrived, so I rowed over in the skiff and picked up a nurse with her medical bag. She had me assist her in getting Paul's clavicle bone back inside his skin and then stitched him up. She gave him some medications for the pain and told us to head for land.

I agreed, but I kept thinking, in the back of my mind that Paul is going to kill me and throw me over the side.

Union workers at Hawaiian Tuna Packers in Honolulu were on strike, so we made our way to Starkist Tuna in San Pedro, California. We first headed straight for Moss Landing to get Paul the medical attention he needed. I slept with a knife and carried it at all times. Paul kept himself heavily medicated and drunk over the next eight to ten days it took us to get to our home port back in Moss Landing, California.

An ambulance came and got him off the boat. In order to get paid, I had to bring the boat to San Pedro and deliver the fish. Paul's brother came with me and we were able to execute the contract.

I weaved the boat through the heavy fog from Moss Landing to San Pedro, avoiding the dozens of offshore oil rigs to deliver our load. I was instructed to bring the boat back to Moss Landing, but after I got my check in San Pedro, I threw all of my gear in my backpack and walked away. I found a local bar, got drunk and checked in to some hotel where I slept it off.

I considered never going back out to sea. It was too dangerous. But at the same time, what else would I do? It was the only way I knew how to make money. How else would I survive?

I guess this is how the world spun. If you got angry, you would lash out, blame others and become violent. I had seen a lot of violence by this point in my life and, in many ways, had accepted the fact that life would be like this forever. I was angry, calloused and my heart was stone cold.

By now, my life lessons were as follows —

- Children get mad and fight with other kids at school.
- Teenagers fight, get high and go to parties.
- Adults get drunk and try to kill each other.
- I was an adult now.

This close encounter with death changed me. It brought to the surface one solid truth: *I valued my life and would fight to the death to preserve it.* I purchased a gun from my weed supplier and began to carry it with me everywhere I went. I figured life was short and I couldn't take the risk of putting my life in the hands of others. But as I carried my weapon around, I asked myself all kinds of questions about my value, and the value of others.

Did I have any value to anyone? Did anyone have value to me aside from my brother and mother? My father(s) didn't. My captain didn't. Was there a greater purpose in life besides survival?

The value individuals place on life varies. Life is largely determined by the purpose one finds in it. If this purpose is self-gratification and personal success, then the value I place on the life of others is diminished or increased by the degree to which their life affects my success or failure.

Should not the value and purpose of life be determined by something much greater than our contribution to society or the machine of financial success?

It sometimes seems to me that the whole world is striving for preservation of life by way of health and wealth—but do we even know why? Do we understand the value of life? Do we know why we are trying to preserve it? I certainly didn't. And still, I perceived there was a reason I was valuable. I intuited there was a purpose for me to be alive. I had heard somewhere before that I had value to God, but could that be possible?

Could God really know me?

If life is so fleeting and temporary, we should seek to find the reason for it, living "all in" for that purpose.

Chapter 7: The Rock in the Storm

The following season, I got a call from a fishing buddy who asked me to work with him on the Feresa, a 73-foot Ketch docked in Honolulu which brought in regular 20-30 thousand dollar loads. I would get 13 percent of the catch and, to make things even better, we would be fishing the fresh fish market. This meant we would only be out for ten to twelve days at a time, as opposed to the six or eight week trips I had been on before.

I felt so fortunate to be able to fish the Feresa so I jumped at the opportunity. I caught the next flight out of Medford, Oregon to Honolulu via San Francisco. I was out to sea within a few days of the initial call.

This fishing expedition reunited me with my good friend Gary. We had fished together since we were young. In fact, he was the one who had gotten me my first fishing job, fresh out of high school, on his grandfather's boat back in Oregon. We made a few trips on the Feresa, made really good money and worked well together as long-time friends.

It was late in the season when the swells began picking up. The South Pacific seas were pulled toward the sky as winds crushed the blue-green translucent water into a frenzy of white chaos. This particular storm was different than countless others I had encountered in the years I had spent at sea fishing commercially. I didn't know how to explain its singularity. I just knew.

No matter where I was fishing, weather was always an issue out at sea. It was the determining factor for how we fished, dressed, cooked, and generally felt on any given day. If the weather was calm and warm, we fished barefoot, shirtless and in a pair of shorts. If the weather was foul and cold, we geared up in full slickers (rain gear), gloves and deck boots.

But something about this approaching storm felt more threatening than the rest. We began making preparations for bad weather, but to be honest, I knew this would be worse than any weather I had seen before.

Everything had to be tied down. The deck needed to be secured, the galley buttoned up and cupboards locked. It was routine foul weather protocol. Gary and I executed the necessary preparations as our captain called out orders. We checked the weather satellite for our area, which looked pretty dangerous, but the three of us had no idea what was really on the horizon.

We had a few thousand pounds of fish on board, packed in ice from our on-board salt water ice-maker, and were several days (about 800 miles NW) from the fresh fish market in Honolulu. We were going to fish the region of the French Frigate Shoals before heading for shore.

The Shoals are a ring-like coral reef that nearly encloses the largest lagoon on the Hawaiian archipelago. This atoll includes over 230,000 acres of reef of which only about 60 are exposed. It is a great place to fish and see marine life (including Great Whites), but due to the 22 miles of shallow, unseen reef, it can also be deadly. Many mariners have lost their lives and vessels here.

The "Janita," a trawler I once fished, sank in these waters. The crew and captain were rescued, along with their dog.

Several hours into what we knew would be a pretty intense storm, we began hearing reports the storm was gaining strength. Some of the other boats on our fleet (of about 40) were getting whipped. One boat, called the "Spirit", had a broken boom and the crew was risking life and limb to secure it before the old wooden boat was torn to pieces. Words like "Category 4" and "hurricane" were heard over the radio.

We were all swearing like the drunken sailors we were, trying to make plans to survive this tempest. We had a huge, risky decision ahead of us. We were close enough to a small pinnacle near the French Frigate Shoals called "La Perouse" we could fight the tide and find shelter in her lei. Our only other option was to risk being thrashed to the sea floor in open waters.

Our Captain decided to risk nearing the Shoals and seeking shelter in the rock.

The problem was that if we neared the Shoals, we were moving toward huge danger. If we got close to the Shoals and, on our approach, the wind shifted, it could throw us right up onto the reef and kill us all. On the other hand, if we could get to the La Perouse pinnacle, we could pull our bow into the lei side of the rock and weather the storm in relative safety.

We could get behind the 120-foot rock, only 350 feet in circumference, and let the rock take the storm. The lei side would provide a small teardrop shape of calm in the midst of the storm. We just needed to get close enough to tuck into the lei of the rock.

The rock was our goal. It promised peace. It promised salvation. But we had to risk everything to make it there.

There are crossroads in all of our lives where high risk in inevitable. Our very survival depends upon the choices we make, and we all need a rock as a refuge from the pending doom of despair. This real-life metaphor of finding the rock of salvation would become a daily reality to me in the near future.

As we fought our way to La Perouse rock over the next several hours, the storm intensified and we continued to question if this was the right call or not. This could be the end of our short lives. Gary and I smoked a lot of weed and talked about death, drowning, girls and God.

I will never forget the calm we found in the lei of La Perouse. We bobbed and weaved our way up close to the rock and, in what seemed like a magical moment, we settled in to the lei. It was beautiful. After many hours of unpredictable chaos and violent thrashing, we made it. We were safe. There was a relative calm and we had shelter from the storm.

If only there were a rock like this where I could find refuge for my life, I thought to myself. Was there a place

I could find this kind of peace and safety internally? I needed that. I needed a place I could drop anchor, a place of safety and refuge, a place of peace.

For the next 72 hours we held our position on constant watch. We could not afford to slip out of the lei and back into the danger of the storm, nor could we lunge bow-first into the rock of our safety. We had to fight to hold our position. Our proximity to the rock determined our fate.

When the nasty storm finally passed, we were able to pull out into the open sea once again with a renewed respect for its power and sovereignty. We made shore a few days later and delivered our fish at the fresh fish market in Honolulu. Once the boat was cleaned, stocked and refueled, we made our way back out to sea, to fill the bowels of the Feresa once again with the Pacific bounty.

I wonder now how many others have been saved by that rock. How many other storms has the rock stood firm against, providing shelter and salvation for the weary and helpless? That rock still remains — immovable, secure, and solid, breaking even the most violent storms. It is a shelter for any and all who need it. To this day, I love that rock and think of it often.

During this season of my life, I was learning new lessons:

- As long as you stay close to the rock, you will find peace, you will be safe, you'll find shelter from the storm.

- The key to your hope and refuge is staying close.
- The rock *takes* the brunt of the tempest yet remains unmoved by its force.

After surviving that raging storm out on the Pacific, I began to consider the possibility of hope. *Maybe I could be rescued. Maybe I could find shelter from rage and guilt.* I wasn't sure yet what that looked like, or what it meant, but I began pursuing a place where I could drop my metaphorical anchor.

Maybe it was religion. Maybe it was a relationship. Maybe it was popularity. Maybe it was as simple as finding love —a family. Whatever it was, I was going to find it. Or maybe it would find me.

Chapter 8: Fisherman

My many years out on the Pacific taught me valuable lessons through trial, error and a lot of pain. Some lessons were learned by my own pain, but others were learned by the pain of someone else.

When we left Honolulu on the Feresa, it would take us a couple of days to get to the fishing grounds where we would bottom fish with hand lines. Bottom fishing was the "meat and potatoes" of our occupation. It wasn't exactly exciting fishing, but it filled the boat with valuable fish and gave us sweet paychecks.

Our fishing grounds were "seamounts" which were between 50-70 fathoms. Seamounts were the tops of underwater mountains reaching miles below to the ocean floor. At the top of the mountains were rock plateaus where fish would school and live in the coral.

To fish these areas, we would move in toward the location and, once we were near, my buddy Gary and I would begin preparing to drop our fishing lines. He would work the station on the starboard side while I would work the port side. We would tie a steel piece of two inch rebar to the bottom of the line and, six feet up from there, we would attach a "palu" bag. The palu bag was a football-sized denim bag with a flap in the top that held chopped anchovies and squid —which would be released in the water at the bottom of the sea when we dropped our lines.

Once the line was set up and baited, we would wait for the captain to position us over the fish he could see on the fish finder.

As soon as we were in the perfect position, the captain would ring the bell and we would drop the weight over the side, complete with the attached palu bag and baited hooks, letting it drop to the floor. When the line went slack as the weight hit the bottom, we would pull up until the line was tight. Then we would pull hard and fast, several times, to get the palu bag to open up and release the chum.

If there were fish down there, they would begin to eat the chum and eventually make their way up to our baited hooks.

When we had a fish on, we would set the hook by hand and wait for another, then another and another. If the fishing was good, we would pull up the line with five fish and do it again.

To reel the fish to the surface, we would use the hydraulic line-pullers. The line-pullers had clutches on them in the event you needed to slow them down or let the line out, even a little. If there was too much resistance, you ran the risk of tearing the hooks out of the fish. However, once the first fish was visible, we would take the line out of the line-puller and "hand line" from there.

We wore hand-made nippers to grab the line so the monofilament wouldn't cut our hands.

Nippers were made of wet suit material and were three inches wide. They slipped over the palm of our hands and went partially down to our second knuckle.

They were a great tool with which to pull the line out because they didn't cover our fingers, which allowed us to get the hooks out of the fish and work without restriction. After a day of wearing nippers while working with salt water, we would have wrinkled, white, dishpan hands that would crack and bleed when they dried out during the night. We would load our hands up with pure lanolin and wear gloves at night to keep the bleeding to a minimum and our hands in good condition.

Once the first fish was on the deck, we would land them on a piece of carpet and kill them with our fish killer. The fish killers were screwdrivers which had been ground to a sharp point. We would drive this sharp point into the top of the spine of the fish, hitting the spinal cord and killing the fish. When you did it just right, they would shiver and die instantly.

Time was critical so we worked quickly to remove the hook, save the bait (if possible) and gently lay the fish in the deck coolers filled with ice brine. The successive fish would be handled the same way and as soon as the last fish from that drop was put in the cooler, the palu bag would be refilled, the hooks baited, and we would hunt for our next location.

While we circled for the next drop, we would transfer the fish into the hold to pack them in ice. This whole process was done at high speed and with great care, so as not to damage the fish in any way. The better looking and fresher the fish were upon delivery, the higher the price we would receive at the auction, which in turn meant more money for everybody. There was a real art to the process.

We made our rounds over the next five or six days and hit the secret fishing spots we had saved in our GPS. Once we reached the end of our eighth or ninth day at sea, we would begin the three-day journey back to Honolulu and deliver our catch at the fresh fish market.

Even when we were in travel mode, we always dragged a few lines behind us to pick up sport fish along the way. Sometimes we would run into a few Mahi Mahi, Ono, Swordfish or even Mako sharks on our way in and out to sea. There were even times we would run into a school of Ahi, adding another $10-20k to our already bountiful load.

We loved hooking up with the sport fish. We would pull these in by hand while one of us took up the slack line on the reels. You never knew exactly what kind of fish it was, or how big it was going to be until it would break the surface and try to shake the hook, which it often did. It was so exhilarating to see these fish fly out of the water on a blue-sky day, even though we already had a full load in our boat.

If the fish hung on and it were too large to pull over the side, we would drop the tailgate. The tailgate had two large through bolts keeping it secure when it wasn't being used. We would pull the bolts in and drop the tailgate down to land a Marlin, Sailfish, really large Ahi or shark. Some of these fish would exceed 400 pounds.

When we were landing a large Marlin or Sailfish, we would wait as the boat surged up and down in the water. In the perfect moment, we would sink our meat hooks into the back of the head of the fish and pull it onto the boat.

A Marlin can easily kill a man with the "steel like spike" on the front of its head, so if the fish thrashed around on board, we were in huge danger. Not only could we be impaled by the spike, but the secondary hook attached to the fish would be swinging around as well, which could grab a fisherman and carry him out to sea. This is one of the main reasons we always kept a knife attached to our belts. If we were ever dragged into the sea by a large fish, we could try to cut ourselves free before we ran out of air.

We were aware of the dangers so, whenever we caught a Marlin, we would bring the spike up to what was termed the Samson Post and tie it off immediately.

The Samson Post was two 4x4 posts mounted ten feet before the tailgate in the center of the deck. These oak posts went through the deck and attached to the keel below deck. They were solid oak and about eight inches apart, specifically designed for this exact purpose. We would pull the Marlin forward and jam his spike between the posts, to avoid being impaled. Then we would tie off the meat hook, binding the fish to the post. As all the adrenaline ran through our bodies, we would immediately cut it and bleed it out, making caveman grunts in light of our victory and preservation of our life and limb.

One time, as we were landing a large bull Mahi Mahi, disaster struck. Scotty, an inexperienced Canadian deck-mate onboard, carelessly got his leg too close. He was hooked in the back of his calf and the Mahi thrashed about before we could kill it. The hook sunk deep into his calf. I tried to hit the fish with a small steel rod we used to stun fish before we killed them, hoping to stop the fish from thrashing. Instead, I hit Scotty's foot, which didn't help matters much. The broken bones in his foot took longer to heal than the hook injury.

The stainless hook was buried deep and went in well past the security barb, which meant there was no way to remove it the way it had entered. We had to push the hook all the way through his leg in a loop-type fashion, cut off the loop on the end and pull it through his leg to remove it. Lesson learned at Scotty's expense.

I learned to avoid the scars borne by countless fisherman by learning from Scotty's accident

Many of us in life are determined to learn the hard way, to learn by making mistakes ourselves. But learning from the experience of others often allows us to dodge pain we would otherwise have experienced. I've learned very few lessons in life by watching and learning from the plight of others. I wish I would have done it more. Most of the big lessons I have learned from in my life have come at my *own* expense.

At this point in my life, I had learned drugs and alcohol were addicting. They had started as my friend, helping to ease the piercing pain I felt in heart. But they eventually became a poison apple, a raging demon that controlled me and fueled my rage, depression and fears.

I had learned unforgiveness and bitterness felt good, particularly since I had very good reason to be angry. These emotions were now consuming me and causing me to become the very person I hated so vehemently. They were ruining all my relationships. My stepfather, who had long forgotten my name, was in many ways still in control of me. I did not yet know how to rid myself of hate but clearly saw its destruction in my life.

I had learned a life consumed with self-gratification was never fulfilled; and the pursuit of money and leisure was a vapor quickly disappearing like the morning mist. There was no way of maintaining its glory.

But mostly I had learned life was dangerous. Either by choice or by default.

Things happen in life that cause pain and it seemed there was no way around it.

Pain was a casualty of life and nobody escaped it.

It had been a few years since I had been in trouble with the law. The last time I was in port I received no injuries from brawling. I had been experiencing a relative calm lately. I was making good money, enjoying life at sea, and working with a good friend who didn't get in my grill. Maybe this was my calling —to be a commercial fisherman. I couldn't think of anywhere I would rather be.

But just under the surface was all the pain and anger. It wasn't gone, just hibernating, only to awaken at some point from its slumber and go on a rampage.

Chapter 9: Clarity

They say there is a time in everyone's life where things start to become clear. There is an intuitive trait in man allowing him to understand how the world turns. Relationships become easier to navigate and maturity sets in.

I am not sure who "they" are, but I have found this concept to be an illusive dream. It seemed as the years went by, the confusion only became greater. Money was not the key to happiness —it fell through my hands like liquid. Relationships came and went without any rhyme or reason. Life continued its rhythmic countdown and it seemed the fog would continue. Periodic clearings would come, but these were only a teaser of hope before the next bank of mist cluttered my mind and dulled my vision.

Was there ever to be a time the sun would shine, without the hopeless knowledge of the temporary? Was there something more to my existence than the next high or the next girl? Was there ever going to be a time when I would find peace...or was life was going to be a constant pursuit of the unattainable? *I had to know.* If there was something, I was going to find it. Whatever it was, I was going to capture it and hang onto it.

Maybe it was health, though I knew no matter how hard I conditioned my body, it would eventually fail me. I would work out for hours everyday while I was out at sea, inventing various routines and changing things up regularly to sculpt my body. I found some discipline in this and my mostly fish diet added to my health. It was a bright spot in life but it ultimately left me wanting.

There was still a longing deep in my soul for something more. Fitness was but a ray of fleeting light in the fog of life.

Money was another pursuit. For a twenty-something young man, I was making plenty of money. I could buy things that were only a dream when I was growing up in Oregon. I paid cash for a nice car, a motorcycle, and nice clothes — whatever I wanted. I knew captains of many of the boats in the fleet and they had plenty of money, homes and cars, but each of them seemed to be trapped in the same fog I was in. No matter how much they had, it wasn't enough. The pursuit went on and on.

I saw the writing on the wall and determined money and the things it could buy were just another one of those elusive dreams of purpose and peace. I kept going down the list of pursuits, trying to discover what I was looking for. But like U2, I still couldn't find it.

Life began to feel like a merry-go-round. I would go out to sea and catch fish, deliver the fish at the fresh fish market in Honolulu, make a ton of money and then go spend it all in Waikiki on whatever felt good. It was euphoric at the beginning of the binge and depressing at the end. Same old thing, same old emotions, same old emptiness.

The highs never felt as high, the girls were never as interested or interesting as the month before, the alcohol was more of a need than a want, and I found myself getting deeper and deeper in debt to all of these things. I thought these things were supposed to make me happy, fulfill my life and give me purpose. It wasn't working out that way. I was becoming numb.

When we were out at sea, that "final call" to drop our lines and pull up the last few fish — an indication from the Captain we were heading to land — was always such an exhilarating release. We knew we had done our jobs. We had a load of fish that would make good money on our return. After packing our final fish in ice in the fish hold, we would double check the whole load to be sure all the fish were looking good and well-covered. We would then make preparations to head for land.

Everything would be rinsed down — the decks scrubbed, dishes cleaned, greasers changed in the engine room and everything stowed in its proper place before we could relax. It would be a couple of days before we would deliver our fish on Oahu or Kauai, so we would take that time to read, sleep, or play the guitar as we set our course. We all took turns on watch in the wheelhouse and kept an eye on the horizon in order to avoid other vessels or large debris.

There would always be a point in our journey where we would keep our eyes on the horizon — land was soon to be seen.

The outline of the islands would be barely visible, to the point where you were not sure if you were really seeing them or not. It was just a light shadow with vague outlines. You could barely distinguish where it began and where it ended. I would look away and then look back to see if I was really seeing land. Sometimes I wanted to see land so badly my mind would play tricks on me. I would think I saw land when I really didn't.

Have you ever wanted something so badly you thought if you stared at it long enough, it would just appear? Or, perhaps you have longed for a relationship so intensely you deceived yourself into thinking you would be fulfilled, content and at peace as soon as it appeared? How about a job, a home, or a position? Whatever it is you are searching for, it is possible to long so intently for something you see things that don't exist. What you see is not what you were looking for.

This had become the story of my life. I was longing for healing in my heart, for purpose. In fact, this had become my relentless focus. I continued to squint and stare at the horizon of life, longing to see something stable and sure.

When you did finally see the islands — when you were sure of it — you would pass the word. We all loved to see land after looking at just the thin horizon of 360 degrees for several weeks. It was a welcome sight. It was so fun to be the one to alert the rest of the crew to its arrival.

Once I saw land, I couldn't take my eyes off of it. It was mesmerizing, hypnotic. It drew me in like sweet music. I would stare at the shadow in the distance and watch it very slowly take shape. It would evolve, at a snail's pace, as it changed from a ghostly outline to an actual formation. I would begin to see where the land ended and the ocean began—just a faint, light grey outline. In time, the view of the land would become crisper and I could see the sketch of the mountains as it morphed from a grey two-dimensional sketch into a colorful third dimension.

It was here the excitement really began.

Once I saw land, I knew it wouldn't be long before I would begin to see trees and waterfalls and the reddish-orange color of the volcanic rocks on the shoreline. Everything would slowly come into focus. The hope I held would soon give way to reality.

At some point we would begin to see movement. If it was an evening approach, we would see lights moving along the roadways. During the day, we would see people playing on the beaches. The buoys at the entrance of the basin would be spotted and soon we would be throwing the lines on the dock, jumping onto land and securing the boat.

If only my life could be like that. I dreamed of a day when I would be able to have that kind of assured hope and clarity; a day when I could get off of the unstable, constantly moving deck and onto solid ground.

Where could I find this kind of security? When could I have it? Did it even exist? My longing for hope in this life was unquenchable —a purposeful void aching to find itself filled.

I needed clarity.

I needed color.

I needed things to stop moving.

I wasn't even sure what clarity looked like. I knew only the grey, two-dimensional life I had been living. I knew it was dissatisfying. I knew there was color and a third dimension. I had just never seen it. Would I ever be able to step off the unstable and drifting deck of life, subject to whatever winds and currents it was caught in? I longed to step off of what I knew as "my life" and just walk away into living color. Was that just a dream or was it really possible? I wasn't sure yet.

There had to be something more than passing days in pursuit of peace, more than just being a slave to the routine of work, more than making money, spending it, and doing it all over again —day after day, week after week, month after month, year after year, until I died. Was this the whole meaning of life, to survive for as long as you can—and then you die?

I needed clarity. It would soon find me.

Chapter 10: Game Changer

Sometimes, we experience monumental moments in life that change the course of our existence. For some, a coach in high school becomes their mentor. For others, it's a tragedy that rocks their world and causes them to take inventory of their lives. Maybe it is as simple as catching a greased pig at a Pioneer round-up or getting arrested for stealing dimes.

I have had a few game changers in life but none compare to the one that altered my life so dramatically and thoroughly as the following. This game-changer was so massive, so monumental — it put me on a trajectory that can only be described as miraculous.

I was between fishing seasons, back in Oregon, visiting my mom and some ex-girlfriends when it all took place.

I was dodging the local cops in Grants Pass for a variety of reasons. I couldn't maintain any kind of long-term romantic relationship due to my short fuse and anger issues. My brother and I hadn't spoken for what seemed like years. My on-again-off-again relationship with an old girlfriend resulted in an unwanted pregnancy and I was scared, depressed and empty. I had plenty of money, a fishing job anytime I wanted in Hawaii, and I owned a nice car. Whoopee!

I was depressed.

My girlfriend and I tried to work it out, but the relationship ended in a tirade of foul words and anger, the finale of virtually every relationship I had ever had.

She eventually miscarried and I never saw her again. I struggled with tremendous guilt over this loss for years.

While I was still numbing my pain with drugs and alcohol, I decided to go to a high school football game at the Grants Pass Downs. Maybe I would run into some old friends. As was my custom, I was pretty lit up when I arrived. Desperately looking for a familiar face so as not to feel alone, I scanned the masses.

I caught the eye of someone with a familiar face but couldn't quite place him. I knew him, but struggled to identify him in my mind. Was he somebody I had done drugs with or otherwise partied with in high school? Perhaps a friend of a friend? Then it hit me: this guy was a Campus Life leader who used to come to my school during lunch and hand out invitations to his clubs. I remember my wrestler buddies and I used to tease him and poke fun at him. He would give it right back to us and seemed like a decent guy. I had actually visited one of his clubs. He needed somebody to stage a fake fight for a crowd-breaker and discussion-starter and I was the most likely candidate.

I made my way through the crowd at the football game and we began to talk. It seemed we had only been talking for a few minutes when I started unloading my life on him. I don't know why, but I trusted him and wanted to tell him about what was going on. He recognized I had been drinking and asked if we could get together the next day and talk. I told him I would like that and he gave me his card with his phone number.

I carried his card around with me for a few days and didn't call him back. I couldn't believe I had been so weak as to tell him about my girlfriend and the pregnancy.

It was late at night, three or four days later, when I was so filled with anxiety and fear I just had to talk with somebody. All the years of hate, anger, pain and regret had worn me thin. I was tapped out and so tired of trying to find peace and purpose in life, only to come up empty. It was as if all the years had culminated in this moment and I couldn't breathe. I was done.

I picked up the phone and dialed the number given to me at the football game. Jeff, the Campus Life guy, answered. I asked if we could connect and as we hung up the phone, he made his way to where I was staying.

We went for a drive that night and he explained to me why I was experiencing what I was experiencing. He explained how sin destroys us —it not only hurts the person committing sin, but everybody around the sinner. Sin has deep roots that spread in every direction, he explained.

I was experiencing the byproduct of living in a sinful world, he continued. My own sin bore down on me in the form of guilt and regret. The sins of my father(s) had hurt me when I was a little boy — abuse and abandonment — and were shaping me into an angry and bitter man. Drugs and alcohol were a way of numbing the pain, but the relief was always temporary.

What I needed was forgiveness and a new lease on life. What I needed was a savior who would save me from myself and from the sin which had torn up my life for so many years. Jeff explained to me how God became a man in the person of Jesus Christ, took the sin of the world upon himself (including mine) and took the wrath of God that was due me for my sin. In other words, Jesus paid the price for my sin.

If I had faith in this work Jesus did on the cross and believed in the irrefutable resurrection of Christ, I could be saved.

Forgiven, fresh start, free from guilt — seriously? I could hardly believe what I was hearing.

As good as it sounded, I was hesitant to fall for this 'Christian thing'. I don't know how many camps or rehabs I was sent to as a kid where I "got saved". The problem was I could never do all the stuff required of me as a "Christian". I would try to be a good Christian for a few days or weeks, but would become exhausted with all the regulations and eventually throw in the towel. I was expected not to go to movies, dance (this was the 80s and disco was in full swing…and yes, I had a mullet), or drink beer (I liked beer). I couldn't go to the lake or river on Sundays because that was church day. Oh, and Wednesday night Bible study was required, so I couldn't go out with my friends that night, either. These were just a few things I couldn't do anymore.

Then there was the list of all the things I had *to* do: I had to read a Bible every day (I wasn't much of a reader…more of a picture guy). I had to go to potlucks, date only church girls (which was a highly restrictive and very shallow pool), pray and give away my money.

This was way too many rules for my taste and, on top of everything else, I was going to inherit another father in the deal —a heavenly father. That was definitely a deal breaker. I didn't need any more fathers in my life.

I shared these frustrations and fears with Jeff that night as we talked. He told me none of that other stuff was part of the deal. If I believed Jesus died for my sin and rose from the grave, he said, I would be saved. I asked him if he was sure and he reassured me several times: "Jim, forgiveness is not something you have to *do*; it is something that has already been done. Jesus did all the work to secure your salvation and forgiveness. You are in perfect standing with God and free of your past. Just believe."

I will never forget that night. I had not cried in over ten years. That night, the dam broke and I cried like the "type A person" I am. *I was all in.* When I cried in the passenger seat of that old Volkswagen, it was as if everybody in Josephine County could hear me. I wept from the deepest part of my soul. I could not believe my fortune. I was forgiven and had a whole new lease on life.

I was in the lei of the Rock. I had found the third dimension, color, and clarity I was looking for. I felt safe for the first time in my whole life. Somebody was watching out for me and placed great value in me. I had a protector and provider —I was forgiven, liberated from the guilt that daily plagued me.

Suddenly, I had purpose in this life. I was no longer searching. I had found what I was looking for. Better said, what I was looking for had *found me*. Even better said, not *what* but Who — *Who* I was looking for — He had found me. It was Jesus. He was the familiar face in the crowd at the football game. He was the Rock in the middle of the Pacific. He was the anchor who steadied my vessel, the clarity on the horizon. He was all these things and so much more. He had been revealing Himself to me all of these years and it all culminated in this moment.

It was the moment faith was expressed. I would never be the same.

I was loved by God. He proved it by dying for my sin, even while I was running from him for all those years. I prayed God would forgive me and I was born again that night. I was given a new heart and a new mind and a new spirit. I now had something to fight for.

> *"And I will give you a new heart, and I will put a new spirit in you. I will take out your stony, stubborn heart and give you a tender, responsive heart."*
>
> — *The prophet Ezekiel*

I was forgiven but not out of the woods yet.

Some say when a man is born again, he can forget the past and move on as if nothing ever happened.

Now that he is a Christian, these folks claim, all those things he used to struggle with are a thing of the past.

I can tell you from experience: this is not so. I still had a very short fuse, still wanted to smoke a lot of pot, still liked the girls. This was so much the case, some would doubt if a true conversion had really happened. I knew I had been forgiven. I actually looked up the verses which declared my salvation through grace by faith in Christ alone. It's true. I was saved! But it would take some time to work out the bugs. In fact, in many ways, I still am working out the bugs.

I went back to fishing in Hawaii, not many months after this experience, and found myself right back in the thick of the world I had come out of. It was a miserable year — I just needed to get out of that world and find a fresh start somewhere else. I went and fished in Alaska for a while but soon ended up just leaving the commercial fishing life altogether.

I worked with Campus Life for a time and went on the road for a year with a rock band named ARC, where I played my guitar. I was now in my mid-twenties and began to actually think about my future for once in my life. I decided the best way to know what God wanted me to do with my life was to learn His Word. So I went to Bible college, which was another game-changer.

After graduating from college, I married Maureen, my beautiful wife, and began raising our son, who was five when we got married. The issues in our marriage started pretty much right after I said "I do".

I had been out of the violent world I grew up in and the crazy violent world of commercial fishing for several years now. I had become a Christian, been to Bible college, and was leading worship at a large church in Southern Oregon. I was supposed to have it all together by now. Right? Well, that was not the case. I was still dealing with anger issues and had zero tools in my bags for how to manage anger or communicate.

When I was a kid, I saw husbands did what they wanted, when they wanted. If it was ever questioned, the wife was quickly put in her place. If she resisted, things became violent. As a fisherman, it was a kill-or-be-killed world. Those were my models. Not surprisingly, those models don't work in marriage, particularly if you are married to an Irish redhead.

Maureen is the best thing that ever happened in my life —other than knowing Jesus —although I was blind to this truth the first year of our marriage. She would stand her ground when I was filled with pride and arrogance, all 110 pounds of her —which infuriated me. This little powerhouse woman could get me so worked up I broke doors, windows, and even bones in my own hand as I would go off on my little tangents of fury. She would have none of my machismo shenanigans and, after a year into our marriage, she moved out with our son to seek solace and protection. At that point, I had some big decisions to make. Either I would get help, or lose my family whom I loved.

I got help.

We had been to multiple marriage counseling seminars and sessions our first year but nothing seemed to help. She just wouldn't change! If Maureen could just see the areas where she needed to change, I figured, we would have a great marriage...right? Wrong. I needed to see how God was changing *me*. I needed to recognize I would never change my wife; and she would never change me. The only thing I had the power to change was myself — and I needed the Spirit of God to make that change.

I was forced to see this the night Maureen left and told me she was not coming back until I got some help. She was not seeking a divorce. That was off the table the moment we got married. But she was rightfully calling me out, saying, "I won't live like this. I won't live in fear. I won't live in this volatile environment. But I love you."

I went to a friend (who seemed to have a good marriage) for advice. I don't remember exactly what he told me that night, but I remember I was finally, for the first time in my life, willing to deal with anger and bitterness that had brewed inside of me for so many years. I opened God's word and read that, to change the way I acted, I needed to change the way I thought.

My *mind* needed transforming and God was able to do that by the power of His Word.

I began to believe God's Word could change me if I believed it and obeyed it—not just as a principle to live by, but as a constant interaction with the Spirit of God and its transforming power in my life. I was determined to think the way God thought and believe He was able to change me. I was able to fight for something that mattered. I was able to fight for my heart now.

*" . . . Fix your thoughts on what is true,
and honorable, and right, and pure, and lovely,
and admirable. Think about things that are
excellent and worthy of praise."*

– The Apostle Paul

That was decades ago and my wife and I are still in the process of that change. But we are also more in love with each other and with Jesus than ever before.

During our second year of marriage, we had an opportunity to move to Mexico and tend to handicapped orphans. We made the move and lived in Carmen Serdan, Mexico for two years before moving to Honduras for a year to help build a Bible school on the Mosquito Coast (appropriately named).

After our three years south of the border, we moved back up to Southern Oregon to continue our journey together in a life of worship as we endeavored to serve God by serving others. My life wasn't perfect, but I now had the mind of Christ, could fight for truth and go on an offensive to protect my new heart, mind and spirit. I could now fight as the warrior God made me to be because the enemy was no longer *others* or myself. I was now able to fight against the enemy of my soul.

I was fighting for the integrity of my own heart and living for the kingdom of God.

Prayer was my battleground. Engaging in battle without prayer as a weapon, I realized, was like being equipped with the most powerful arsenal—sure to defeat the enemy—and never using it. Many disciples of Jesus are living defeated lives due to their unbelief in the power of prayer.

I would drop anchor here, in the Word of God, and in prayer. Permanently. It would be the compass I would use with which to get my bearing in life. I would recheck my course regularly.

Life finally had meaning and purpose. I would no longer spend my days searching or simply existing. I would live life *now*. This is where the adventure really began for me, in living color. I had found my true North.

Chapter 11: Climbing Higher

There are a lot of different sports one can be involved in —all are good for the spirit and build strength, teach perseverance or provide the shot of adrenaline you need. However, in my experience, rock climbing tops them all.

My first time out rock climbing was at Smith Rocks State Park, just outside the little town called Terrebonne near Bend, Oregon. Smith Rocks is a rock canyon that stretches for miles with a beautiful river running through it. There are over 1000 bolted climbs for the sport climber to use as well as hundreds of pro climbs.

My first lead climb was on a large boulder called "rope de dope" in 1990. I was 26-years old and speaking at a high school camp for the week. Part of our week-long adventure included cycling portions of the Oregon coast and traveling over to Smith Rocks to climb.

I started with a "top rope" set-up where the lead climber would set the rope through chains at the top of the route and then rappel his descent. Once he was back on the ground, the lead climber would tie me to the opposite end of the rope and belay me as I climbed. He would take up the slack as I made progress and, in the event I fell, the rope would immediately tighten and stop the fall. It was a rush. Even though I believed the rope would hold me, it took real faith to actually feel comfortable with it.

When you are hanging 50 or 60 feet off the ground and only have a 10 millimeter rope between you and the ground below, your prayers are never more sincere.

I was so enthralled by the sport after that first time, I began to train and make regular trips to local climbing areas in the Rogue Valley — places like Rattlesnake, Cathedrals, and Emigrant Lake. I did my first three-pitch pro climb at Castle Crags in Northern California in 1998. It was a real victory, but I still had a longing to climb the famous Monkey Face at Smith Rocks.

Monkey Face is a rock column that towers above the NW side of Smith Rock canyon. It is a 350-foot column of rock that is very technical and requires great skill to climb. The approach to Monkey Face involves a short hike along the river and passage through a saddle until you reach the face of the rock.

The first pitch (section of the climb) is relatively easy, but you enter the face of the rock at 55 feet above ground. Right out of the gate, you are in the dead zone. No mistakes allowed. Mistakes could be deadly.

The first pitch is nubby and has plenty of quarter-sized and dime-sized nubs where you can smear your rubber soles, gain traction and move up. Once you've led the first pitch, you belay fellow climbers from the top of the pitch.

We trained hard and planned this epic climb for months. Every pitch was studied and every technical move was mastered. We were ready for the climb. My climbing partners and myself were going to defeat Monkey Face.

We all made it to the little patio at the top of the first pitch and regrouped. It was about 9:00am and we were all pumped to be there. Nothing else mattered at this point. Everything had to be pushed out of our minds so we could concentrate on the next pitch, which was 60 meters.

The second pitch was the technical part of the climb. On the western face of the rock, there was nothing to climb. It was sheer rock face, impossible to climb without assistance. Bolts had been placed on this face in a series, each about eight feet apart, creating a vertical line to the mouth of the monkey.

Once in the mouth, you were no longer exposed and would be over half way up the climb.

As you ascend the bolt ladder, you must use a daisy chain and an ascender. The daisy chain is a leash, which you can clip into the bolt and use to step yourself up. After securing yourself with another leash, you can release the daisy chain, reach for the next bolt, and go through the process all over again as you ascend to the mouth. It is a relatively simple process, but you don't get to make any mistakes.

It took a few hours for all three of us to make it into the mouth of the Monkey. This was the crux of the climb. We had read the climbing manual and talked with those who had gone before us and knew this was the point where we had to reach into the unknown. In order to continue up, you had to step out on a ledge that dropped off over 200 feet, reaching out and up over your head.

There you would find a "thank God hold," and you would know you were home free. But that hand-hold could only be found after you fully committed. It was about a foot out of reach and you couldn't see it, so in order to land this hold, you had to lunge and trust it was there. I am trembling just writing about it.

I was the first one out of the mouth and lunged for the hold. I stuck it ("thank God") and continued the climb to the next patio, where I would belay my partners up.

Not long after this, we made the summit, shouted our caveman grunts in victory, and began to plan our safe descent off this rock.

Rappelling off this type of rock is tricky. The bottom of the rock is well beyond the reach of your rope, so you have to rappel to a safe point, clip into the rock, pull your second rope out of your bag, set up another rappel and continue down, all the while leaving your partner enough rope to complete their rappel.

It takes time, thought, planning — you must keep your cool.

We were all standing on the first rappel point on our chosen ledge and I began to set up the gear. At one point, we were all a bit cramped and I decided I needed to get to the other side of Scott. He would stay clipped in while I would step around him and clip *back* in, making sure to keep the safety leash secured.

We had been on the rock six hours now and I was feeling mentally fatigued. Mental fatigue in this type of climb is what is most dangerous.

I stepped around Scott and continued throwing ropes and setting up the rappel.

After getting things set up, I reached for my safety leash to unclip myself and begin my rappel. That's when I realized: I was unclipped! Somehow I had neglected to clip back in after stepping around Scott. For the several minutes it took to set up the rappel, I was completely exposed. If I had I lost my balance at any point during that set-up, I would have fallen to my death.

When I realized what I had done, I felt sick. I thought about life and how short it really is. I thought about how quickly mine could have ended. I was mad at myself for being so absent-minded and mad at my partners for not checking my gear. We had some words there on the rock but, at the end of the day, we all got our feet back on the ground and considered the climb a great success.

At some point in life, we all die. Be it a car accident, cancer, old age, or an absent-minded rock-climbing mistake ten out of ten of us die. There's a 100% certainty you're not going to make it. But of course an experience like this makes you wonder:

- How do I want to die?
- How much control do I have over my life and death?

It makes you take the whole thing more seriously.

Despite my near-death experience, climbing was in my blood; and since the winter months prevented me from sport climbing, I began to gear up for high-altitude mountaineering.

At 14,179 feet, Mount Shasta towers above the Southern Cascade mountain range. It is an intimidating fixture rising out of the flatlands that are filled with hummocks in Northern California. Only an hour south of the Oregon border, this mountain always intrigued me as a kid. I would pass by it on periodic Greyhound trips down to Los Angeles to visit my Dad.

My first opportunity to take the summit came in 1995, with a friend who was a ranger in the Grand Titans for many years and had also spent a few years as a climbing guide on Mt. Shasta. We had taken several trips over to Smith Rocks to climb and, as we discussed our climbing adventures, he mentioned his adventures on Mt. Shasta. I immediately asked if he would guide me up to the summit. He quickly agreed and I made my first ascent up to the summit that year.

The ascent became an annual event for me. Over the years, along with other mountaineers, I would plan and execute many different routes to the top.

The first few years we took the traditional route, through Avalanche Gulch, known as the John Muir route. Once we checked in at the ranger station in Mt. Shasta City, purchased a summit pass, and received our waste carry out bag, we made for the trailhead at Bunny Flats at 6,500 feet.

We checked our route, secured our packs, and began our trek to Horse Camp, a stop only a few miles up through the tree line where an artisan spring bubbles with pure, sweet water to fill our reservoirs. That's where the real climb begins.

After the tree line ends, you are totally exposed. There are no shelters, no trees, and no running water up to the summit and back.

One of the amazing and scary things about Mt. Shasta is that it can create its own weather. There were times we experienced a complete whiteout within a matter of minutes. The clouds would form so quickly — at one point you would have perfect visibility and the next moment you wouldn't even be able to see your feet. When this happened, your only option was to rally together by following the voice of the guide; then you would hold until the weather cleared or dig in and set up camp for the night.

On one expedition, my team and I were climbing the North Slope in groups of three. We were all tied to one another, about five meters apart, because we were on solid ice. We had to climb above a major crevasse, about 100-feet deep.

Crevasses are deep holes in the ice which form razor sharp edges along their inner walls. The last thing you want to do is fall into a crevasse. If the fall itself doesn't kill you, you will most likely die from lacerations, as you can bleed out before you have a chance to be rescued. Therefore we tied ourselves together above the crevasse. In the event one of us slipped and began to slide, the other two could immediately collapse onto the ice, self-arresting by digging our ice axes in preventing a tumble to our inevitable death.

We crossed the top edge of the crevasse at around 4:00am, just as the sun was beginning to show its light. The stars were out and the ice crystals were thick in the air. It was nothing less than otherworldly. Just beyond this crevasse is the Humboldt glacier and icefall. There, you can look into the translucent blue ice that has been frozen for centuries.

After this, it is a long, agonizingly steep climb to the summit.

Once a climber gets above 12,000 feet, all kinds of mental games begin. Many times, in the thin air at those high altitudes, I have asked myself, "Why am I doing this? What am I up here for?" Everything within you begins to gasp. The air gets thinner and thinner and, with every step, breathing becomes more difficult. Altitude sickness can kick in at any moment.

I have wandered off the main route to empty my queasy stomach and been left wanting for enough energy to manage another step. You never know when this type of sickness will overcome you, but you must press through it.

One time, up above Misery Ridge (appropriately named) at about 13,000 feet, I noticed a lone climber lying down behind a large rock to the East of me. I made my way over to him. He was completely delirious and making no sense with his words. He sounded drunk. This is a common symptom of altitude sickness and is highly dangerous. Bad decisions can be made when you're not thinking clearly. As I tried to help him out, I finally understood he was with a party in front of us. He had gotten sick and the others in his party told him to wait there as they made for the summit. I secured him with a line, made sure he was warm and had water, and then found his party on the summit. I told them I was glad I didn't have friends like them.

You never leave a delirious climber alone.

Mental exhaustion can cause you to make mistakes that could cost you your life. I have seen mountaineers simply forget to take off their crampons during a glissading attempt and, the moment they put their foot down to slow their descent, they launch into a death tumble.

Glissading is a technique used to descend the mountain at high speeds. If the conditions are right and you are prepared, you can cut hours out of a descent by carefully removing your crampons, sitting down on the ice, and sliding down feet-first. Your ice axe is used as a rudder, both to direct your downward path and act as a brake when you get beyond a comfortable speed.

On Mt. Shasta this technique can be practiced for a quick, 30-minute passage through the heart of the mountain to Lake Helen. In contrast, descending on foot takes around two hours. I have never actually seen a climber die, but I have been *on* the mountain when other climbers have lost their lives. One died of a heart attack and the other attempted to glissade with his crampons on —he was impaled by landing on his ice axe. Mountaineering is a high risk sport.

Another danger zone on Mt. Shasta is the climb through the Red Banks. These chutes of ice are formed between vertical rocks along the west side of the Mountain at about 12,000 feet. It can be treacherous and it is wise to secure a line to climb through the chutes.

I was climbing up through the main chute a few years ago when another climber, ten feet above me, lost his footing and slid toward me so quickly I barely had time to jump over him as he skidded by. I tried to grab him as he raced by, but was unable to hang onto him. He tumbled and broke several bones before he came to a stop over 1,000 feet down the mountain. The medics were called in to lift him out.

Accidents can happen fast. You must maintain mental alertness and not allow yourself to get sloppy in your foot placement.

I was always on high alert during my first few major summits, checking and double-checking my gear. After I became familiar with climbing, as in other disciplines, I had the tendency to become over-confident and sloppy. This was as much of a danger as inexperience.

Preparedness is also a key factor for survival. I would always go through my gear in my living room several days before a summit in order to check and re-check my gear. In the event of an emergency or foul weather, the items you bring with you can be a matter of life or death.

One year, we were caught in a heavy, wet snowstorm on Shasta. It was one of those storms where the weather was not extremely cold, but the snowflakes were huge and sticky -- this meant any unprotected area of your pack or skin was immediately wet. I had been putting off getting a new pair of high altitude gloves, which was a huge mistake for this trip. My gloves had seen better days, and I knew that, but didn't want to spend the money.

I thought I could get away with the old gloves for one more year. Bad call.

My hands got wet and frostbite began to numb my fingers in a matter of minutes. We quickly dug in and got our shelter up, but by the time I was inside and in my sleeping bag, my body had entered the first stages of hypothermia. I was shivering uncontrollably and I couldn't feel my hands. The group quickly boiled some water and I eventually warmed up with four or five cups of hot chocolate and top ramen. It was a scary experience and I learned my lesson well.

If you don't have the right gear, you don't get on the mountain. Preparedness is vital.

The descent is always the most dangerous part of the climb. At altitude you never feel good. Headaches, joint pain and nausea always accompany high altitude. Once you have conquered the summit, your goal is to get down the mountain as quickly as possible. You feel a noticeable improvement in how you feel for every 500 feet you descend, so you want to hurry down. This can be done safely but you must always be thinking. You must be aware of the dangers and keep a level head. 80% of injuries happen on the descent.

Preparedness, training, and focus are all vital to success. Above all, you must be careful how you walk and where you walk.

Life is like this. We all are on a journey with danger at every turn. If we are not prepared and aware of those dangers, we will fall and be injured or killed. Preparation and planning are key. We must approach our journey with eyes wide open, knowing the dangers, and being ready to sidestep them when they arrive.

We must have the right gear and knowledge to live, no matter the circumstance.

If we are not prepared, we are subject to the harsh, and sometimes deadly, fury of our circumstances.

These are the lessons I gleaned at this point in my spiritual journey. This is what the mountain taught me — ultimately, circumstance (just like weather) is outside of our control. But how we plan for and manage our circumstances matters. We have so many choices and what we choose makes a difference. As on the mountain, I should expect difficulty, trauma and change in my life. *Am I prepared for it?*

> *"By His divine power, God has given us everything we need for living a Godly life. We have received all of this by coming to know Him, the One who called us to Himself by means of His marvelous glory and excellence."*
>
> *— The Apostle Peter*

There is a level of fitness that is required if we are going to be at all productive and successful in our life as a disciple of Christ. I can plan and prepare with tedious detail, but if I have not spent any time training, I am doomed to fail. We can choose to stay at the bottom of the mountain, but a decision to climb requires obedience, training and faithfulness.

We prepare for this climb called 'life' by knowing Jesus, our guide who tells us exactly which way to go and how to get there. His instructions might not make sense to us at the time, but we have to listen and trust He knows the way. We prepare for this life by knowing God's Word, which in turn reveals His character. We plan our journey by making the time to open the scriptures regularly, allowing God's Word to wash over us, refresh us, revive us, restore us, prepare us, and shape us into the image of Christ.

Chapter 12: Risk

I got the call late at night.

It was an invitation from a friend to go paddle rafting on the Cal Salmon River in Northern California. I had never been through class five rapids and this stretch of river had a few of them. An experienced paddle rafter on the crew had an emergency and couldn't make the trip, so I was called in as a rookie back up. I had no idea what I was getting myself into, but I'm always up for adventure — of course I was in.

We were leaving early the next morning, so I had to make some quick scheduling adjustments. Without much effort, we were on the road at 4:00 am.

When we arrived at the river later that morning, I was instructed in my role as part of the paddle raft team. Dale Hosley was our guide. He had years of experience as a river guide and owned a company which regularly made trips down the Lower Rogue Canyon, known as *The Wild and Scenic*.

I trusted him completely and knew he would guide us safely down this river.

I quickly learned the commands he would yell, and what I was supposed to do when he yelled them. I was ready for the adventure.

We made our way down the first few (class three and four) rapids. It was intense. The scenery was spectacular, the water was cold and our lifejackets were secured. There came a point where we were approaching the big rapids — affectionately named "Freight Train" and "Last Chance". The journey through these obstacles would also prove to be an unforgettable, dream-worthy experience for years to come.

As we approached "Freight Train," we pulled over to the side and walked down the river to get a look at it. I could not believe my eyes. Fear ran through me, but I suppressed it, acting excited to 'shoot' through this monster. Mind you, I had never paddle rafted before. I had taken a one-man, inflatable Tahiti through the Hell's Gate Canyon on the lower Rogue River and had been through some class fours, but this one was way bigger than anything I had seen.

Dale made some mental notes about how the river was reacting and we ran back up, getting back in the raft. You could feel the power of the water and hear it roar on our approach. We got into the rapid and began to yell and scream with excitement. We were *in it*. We were alive and hanging on for dear life.

At one point, I glanced back and saw Dale in the water. He yelled for me to grab him and I was able to reach out and pull him back into the raft. Fred, who was in the front left station (operative word being "was") was now in the water too. Once he was in, he took off down the river, bobbing in and out of sight. He was an experienced oarsman who knew to keep his feet forward and not fight the current. We eventually caught up with him and got him back in the boat.

It was a rush. We continued safely down the river.

This trip would prove to be good experience, as I would find myself years later with the opportunity to float down the White Nile River in Uganda, Africa. I was leading a group of 42 people on a missions trip to Africa. We were in Africa to accomplish three objectives: share the Gospel with thousands of children by performing open-air drama and music, provide food to their starving bodies and lead a pastor's conference. We fed hundreds at a time as we gave them the life-giving message of Christ and the power of the cross.

Uganda is filled with millions of children who have no parents or adult relatives due to the high mortality rate (greatly influenced by the AIDS virus). Wherever you look in Uganda, there are hungry children. Of course, feeding a fraction of these children and sharing the Gospel with them only scratched the surface of the problem, but we should always do what we can.

At the pastor's conference, the other leaders and I taught through the book of Romans. We were able to teach the Word to over 400 pastors. We still continue this type of work in India and Nepal.

Near the end of our two-week trip, I had planned to take all who were interested rafting down the White Nile. We hired a rafting company in Jinja to guide us down the river. They were all professional and well-trained guides. They gave us the option to float down different lines in the rapids— extreme, moderate or mild.

I had to take the extreme boat. My wife got in one of the moderates while others took the mild.

When you float such a huge river with multiple class five rapids, even the mild lines are intense. Of course, being in the "extreme" boat meant we would find the most difficult and shoot through them with the real possibility of flipping the boat (which we did, several times).

We went right through 'Bujagali Falls', 'Overtime' (which is a 4.5 meter waterfall), and also 'The Bad Place' — all of which are extreme class fives. The sheer volume of water in this river is nothing like what you would see in Oregon or Northern California. The White Nile is like taking 50 Rogue Rivers and pouring them into one giant one.

As we reached the top of "Overtime," I was launched out so quickly I had no idea what had happened. Before I knew it, I was swallowed up in this white-water current and had no idea which way was up. I held my breath and curled up as instructed, waiting to surface. It felt like I was in a washing machine and was quickly running out of air. I knew at any moment I would pop through this nightmare and get some oxygen. Any second now...

My lungs were burning and body tingling — fear gripped my soul. I broke free from the fetal position I was told to stay in and began flailing for the surface. I needed air. *Right now*. Just then, I saw the surface and broke through, with a gasp for air that never tasted so good. I am pretty sure I held my breath for at least an hour. Maybe two.

All of us had similar stories and yet we all made it through alive. It was the experience of a lifetime.

Great experiences usually require high risk. Wouldn't you concur?

These days, I'm learning to see how life is like this. Living a life of faith means high risk is inherent. But our perspective of risk is largely dependent upon our understanding of God's faithfulness. If we don't believe God is one hundred percent faithful, one hundred percent of the time, we will live in fear, never stepping outside of what is comfortable. We will be greedy and small.

On the other hand, if we believe in the absolute faithfulness of God, we will obey at any moment. We will risk absolutely everything to follow his lead because we *know* He will forever be faithful to carry us, no matter how "high risk" things may seem. I am not saying we should take unnecessary risks. I am saying, when God speaks, obey Him. Immediately. Don't wait until it seems logical. Obey Him now. He is faithful. He will keep you. Trust Him.

> *Faith is the confidence that what we hope for will actually happen; it gives us assurance about things we cannot see.*
>
> *- The Writer of Hebrews*

Living a life of faith requires complete abandonment of what is safe and reasonable. Once you live this way, trusting in the faithfulness of God, you will be forever ruined for 'normal.' I have been ruined for normal. I pray you are ruined, too.

God did not place us on this earth to pursue the American Dream. God placed us here to glorify Him and our mission is to make disciples. Our life is not about us. It is about *Jesus*. And we have the choice. We can either live "all in," making disciples and living for the kingdom of God, or we can live for our own Kingdom, ending our days in regret as we realize the insignificant nature of the life we chose.

When we live a life of faith — fully receiving the generosity of God's grace and mercy — we become a conduit of His generosity. That means our pool of resources for love, joy, peace, patience, and kindness is never-ending. We can love our neighbors with total abandon and trust God for the outcome. As the Spirit of God prompts us, we can risk everything, reach for the astronomical, and defy laws of this world because we are citizens of another world entirely.

Live with purpose. Enjoy the journey. Love with passion. Laugh really loud. Feed the hungry. Help the hurting. Live outside your cubicle and take risks. After all, life is dangerous anyway. So live loud.

Chapter 13: Deliverance

I caught the bug to travel and help others in my mid-twenties and it has been a part of my DNA ever since. I have had the privilege of traveling to serve in multiple countries including Mexico, Honduras, France, Ireland, Israel, Russia, Ukraine, Germany, England, Wales, Nepal, India, Africa, Australia, Fiji, and Vanuatu in the South Pacific.

One year, while in India, I was teaching at a pastor's conference. We spent time going into unreached villages to bring medical aid to the natives. It was in one of those villages where I was confronted with a scene that would forever change my worldview.

We had traveled by van for several days to the trailhead where we threw our packs and supplies into the back of a huge truck and began our ride up the rainforest trail. We spent seven hours in the truck until we reached a point where we could literally go no further. Then we hiked the remaining distance to our destination.

At the end, there was a village named "Krishna, Krishna" where we set up our medical clinic. We carried in hundreds of pounds of much-needed supplies, rice, and wool blankets to the locals in this highland area. We were there for several days and word got out to the surrounding farmers about the "white medics" in the village. New villagers began to arrive at our portable medical clinic.

At the end of our last day there, I was asked by one of the young Indian gals to come to her home. She told me her father was in trouble—he had been possessed by a demon for years—and needed help. I prepared for what I was about to witness. I grabbed a few team members and brought them to the hut I was asked to visit. We met the mother of the young Indian gal who had requested our presence and help.

After formal introductions, she told me her husband had been possessed for years and asked if we could help him. The town leader was present and told us the possessed man would burn down homes and was very violent. They'd eventually had to lock him in a dungeon of sorts, where he'd been for the past four years...four years!

There was a heavy chain securing the thick door, with only a small slit through which they would slide his food. I asked for the key, unchained the door and ducked as I went inside. My eyes adjusted to the darkness, and there I saw a figure on the damp dirt floor. He hardly looked dangerous.

As things came into focus, I saw a man lying in his own waste, with his hands bound behind his back and one leg also tethered. He was stiff and crying.

I picked him up and brought him into the light. I had never seen a human being in worse condition.

I began to untie the ropes that had grown *into* his swollen and infected arms. The locals backed away and started yelling at me not to untie him. Meanwhile, I was thinking: *He is less than a hundred pounds. How dangerous could this guy be?*

I continued peeling off his restraints and the medics with me ministered aid to his open and infected wounds. As we took off his filthy and refuse-caked clothing, we found he had a serious abscess on his backside. The medics opened up the abscess and the black and yellow fluid poured from his body — it was beyond description. The stench... it was unbelievable.

As we cleaned his wrists, we found the copper bracelet he was wearing had dug so far into his arm it couldn't be seen until the first layer of sickness was removed. We had to dig into his arm to cut off the bracelet. We literally had to scrape the wound clear before we could actually see it. A witch doctor had told him to keep this copper bracelet on to ward off evil spirits. If he removed it, the witch doctor assured him he would die.

The guy was a mess.

Even in all this pain, the man managed to stand up and spit on us, yelling and screaming. He manifested demons and did totally unnatural things with his body. I prayed for deliverance and called upon Jesus to deliver this poor man from the enemy who had taken control of him. After a few minutes of prayer, he fell down and went totally limp.

I thought he had died. Just then, he opened his eyes and, with a calm voice, looked at his wife and asked for something to eat. She cried and brought him food.

Just like that, we witnessed a man be delivered from years of possession. The man sat in the sunshine and we talked. I spoke the Gospel of grace and hope to him. He said he wanted this Jesus. He wanted freedom. We prayed with him and he placed faith in Christ. He believed *Jesus* would enable him to forever be free from the demons that had plagued him for so many years.

As I told him goodbye, he pleaded with me not to leave him. He didn't want to be subjected to the fear and torture he had been a slave to over the past four years. I told him he was free now, that God would never leave him. He had been delivered by a power greater than what possessed him previously. Now that he had Jesus inside him, there was no room for any evil spirits.

He smiled and said thank you, a "thank you" unlike any I had heard before.

After we left, we used the resources from our church to purchase a motorcycle for a pastor to be able to get back and forth from the village to preach the Gospel. Since this first contact with the unreached village, the entire village has come to faith in Christ. The little Hindu Temple has been dismantled and a thriving Jesus Church is growing and strong.

Deliverance comes in all shapes and sizes.

Most of us have never seen the scene I just described, but have perhaps experienced some other kind of bondage that hides behind a smiling face. Drugs, alcohol, pornography, food, relationships, hatred, bitterness — no matter how we slice it, hidden or obvious, we all need deliverance from the chains of the enemy that bind us and choke us out. I'm no different. I've known the pain of addiction and entrapment. Now I know that freedom — true freedom — which can only be found in Jesus.

Nothing can deliver us from our past of brokenness, our addictions, our bitterness, our hatred and guilt but Jesus.

We can certainly numb ourselves to the presence of such pain or be temporarily distracted through some erotic experience; at the end of the day, however, true freedom only comes when we surrender our whole selves to the life-altering, heart-changing love of God through Christ.

Chapter 14: Provision

It was 1989. My beautiful wife and I had been married for only six months when we made a trip with some good friends to a three day concert/conference in Washington State called Jesus Northwest. As a musician and songwriter, I always enjoyed concerts, seeing new bands and hearing new songs.

We made our way up the I-5 corridor to the venue and had a great few days with our friends, Dave and Jenni. It was on the journey home when something happened which would prove to be another landmark moment, altering the course of my life.

We were driving south on our way back home when I mentioned something I was thinking. One of the speakers, by the name of Josh McDowell, just returned from Romania and was speaking about the opportunity to share the Gospel in countries that had been previously hostile to the Gospel. There was such a sense of urgency to what he was saying —the window was open *right now* but wouldn't be open for long.

Dr. McDowell proceeded to challenge the audience: if the Lord was calling anyone to go, now was the time to believe God and trust Him for provision. If God was calling *you* to go, he was saying, He would provide the resources and make all the arrangements. It was time to trust God and obey.

One thing in particular stuck in my mind from what he said. Dr. McDowell said, "if you are a

Christian and wear 501 jeans, you are equipped to preach the gospel." People of Eastern Europe, he explained, are so infatuated with people from the West, they will listen to anything you have to say. Use what you have and share the gospel.

I remember looking down and seeing the 501s I was wearing at the time.

I could not get this out of my mind. I felt as though I was actually hearing from God; and in that case, I needed to respond.

I told Dave, Jenni and Maureen what I was feeling. Dave about came out of his skin and told us he had felt the same thing. We talked about driving my old split-window 63 VW bus up through Alaska and loading it on a ferry across to Siberia where we could travel through Russia, sharing the gospel. It was one of the most harebrained ideas ever brewed up, but all of us (including our wives!) were just crazy enough to attempt it.

We all moved into a small apartment together in Medford to save money and finalize our plans. During this time together, Dave's wife Jenni became pregnant and they decided the Lord was redirecting them. I wondered if I was to abort the mission, too, but thanks to the encouragement of my wife, I stayed my course.

It turned out I *did* end up going to Eastern Europe, but not via VWs and ferries.

I soon met a man who had defected from the Ukraine and was now a US citizen. He lived in Ashland, only 30 minutes from my home, and he wanted to go back to the Ukraine to visit. He didn't want to travel alone and was willing, if I travelled with him, to act as my interpreter.

At the time, I was climbing trees for a living in the Tioga unit between Eugene, Oregon and the Pacific coast. I was winning bids on government jobs, which meant I would go out into the forest for weeks at a time. Gearing up with spurs and a flip line, I maintained trees that pickers would climb for cones. They would use the cones to harvest the seeds for reforestation. My job was to put steel pegs into the trees so the pickers could get up the trees, without spurs. I would also limb dead branches and clear the ground around the base of the trees.

I had been out in the woods for a few weeks, wondering how the Lord was going to provide the money and time for me to be able to complete the mission to the Ukraine and share the gospel.

There were few cell towers in this area at the time and cell phones were rare, so my only contact with my wife was when I came out of the woods and found a pay phone. I remember the first conversation after two weeks of no contact. She told me how the Lord had provided a plane ticket for me to Frankfurt, Germany, and from there, train tickets through Germany, Poland and into the Ukraine. God answered my prayer and I couldn't believe the way He provided, right down to the smallest detail.

I was beginning to recognize that a life serving Jesus with radical abandonment was a great adventure. I was going to the Ukraine to share the gospel with the host of lost souls who needed to hear God's message.

Just before I left, I received a call from a man who had somehow heard I was going to the Ukraine. He told me he had in his possession — about a hundred Ukrainian Bibles — and wanted to know if I would like to bring them with me. The answer was obvious. A few weeks later, I was on a plane with my friend Dmitri, my guitar, and a hundred Ukrainian bibles.

I was excited, prepared and unashamed.

We landed in Frankfurt, Germany early October of 1990. It was one of the greatest times in German history. The Berlin wall was being dismantled and East Germans were flooding into West Germany.

Germany was unified as a fulfillment of a dream that began in the middle of the 19th century.

After landing in Frankfurt, we hopped a train and headed toward Poland, where we would cross the border in Peremysh. In order to obtain visas into the Ukraine, we needed to stay the night in a hotel in Warsaw and show our passports. This leg of the journey would become one of the most unforgettable moments in all my travels.

On the flight over from the States, Dimitri and I met a man named Steve, who happened to be traveling the same route as us and was continuing to Moscow. In the course of our conversation, we found we all had matching tickets through Warsaw and into the Ukraine, so what started as a traveling pair now became a traveling threesome.

Steve, Dimitri and I found the train station in Frankfurt to be a massive structure that accommodated dozens of trains simultaneously with "to-the-second" accuracy (the European train system is the most reliable and accurate on the planet). We entered this massive station, found our train and boarded. We jammed our luggage in the same cabin, along with my guitar, and were excited to be on the next leg of our journey.

Every few hours, the train entered into another massive station where it would pause for a short time to drop off and reload passengers. One stop found us in the Leipzig station and, since Dmitri was asleep, Steve and I took the opportunity to run to the end of the dock and grab a quick espresso and pastry. That's when the unthinkable happened.

I glanced back and saw our train beginning to move. I yelled for Steve and ran down the dock to hop back on the train as I had done so many times before, in Mexico, but this train was different. The doors were all hydraulically operated and closed up tight. There was no room between cars to jump on. Steve and I watched as our train pulled out of the station and, eventually, out of sight.

Dmitri was still on the train, no doubt fast asleep, along with our luggage. We had no cell phones. We also had no plan. I knew to always keep my money and passport on my person, so at least I had some cash. Steve, on the other hand, had nothing on him.

We ran outside the station and tried to find a taxi driver who spoke English. After finding one and haggling over the cost of bringing us to the next train stop, we hopped in and had our first experience on the European autobahn: no speed limits.

The train beat us to the next stop, so we quickly shot for the border, where we hoped to meet up with Dimitri... and our luggage... and my guitar!

After dishing out a couple hundred dollars at the border of Germany and Poland, we began our search for Dimitri. We waited for our scheduled train to arrive, having beaten it to the border by only half an hour. I got excited as it approached. Steve and I waited, anxiously anticipating the moment when Dimitri would disembark with our luggage. But the train came and left: no Dimitri, no luggage, no guitar.

We waited all through the night, checking each train to see if he got off and then got back on another train. It was about 3:00am when we finally saw Dimitri dragging our luggage off a train. We ran to him, helped him with the luggage, and hugged him. I was never so glad to see my little Jewish friend!

Come to find out, he had awakened shortly after we disembarked in Leipzig and, after searching for us on the train to no avail, he simply got off at the next stop and waited for us to come find him. He thought to himself, "How stupid would Jim be if he didn't just go to the next station and look for me?" Well.

We finally got through the border and into Warsaw and, from there, into the Ukraine. It was a wild ride. I love wild rides —when they're over!

Once we settled at the grandmother's house of an old friend of Dimitri's, I filled my days by going to the parks and university campuses, playing my guitar. Large crowds would gather as I played and sang; Dimitri would interpret, not only what I was singing about, but also the Gospel as I presented the truth to all who would listen. Many asked how they too could be saved. It was the beginning of what would later become a lifestyle.

I had been frequenting the University for awhile when I was invited to the arts class to sing and do a little mini-concert. I was amazed at the openness and invitation. I was actually able go into the class, filled with students, to sing and share the Gospel. The people of Ukraine were hungry and open!

After a few weeks of ministry in Lvov, I stumbled upon a gathering in the courtyard of the University and walked over to see what was up. There was a group of Christians selling Bibles. I had the money to purchase the table full of Bibles, as well as the remainder in the boxes under the table, and began to hand them out for free. Suddenly, there was a scramble in the crowd. Everyone wanted to get their hands on a Bible.

One very large Russian man approached me and asked what I was doing, who I was, and why I was giving out Bibles. As Dimitri translated, I could sense his uneasiness about this man and his desire to just get away from the whole scene. I, on the other hand was intrigued and wanted to talk with the man further. Finally, the large man said he wanted Dimitri and I to come with him to meet his pastor. I agreed. Dimitri, on the other hand, was not so willing.

When Dimitri had defected 11 years earlier to the United States through England, the KGB was a dominant force in the Ukraine and would intervene if more than three or four people gathered in the streets.

The Church was under great persecution then. So Dimitri was extremely hesitant to get into a car with this guy. I had to drag him along with some fierce language to get him to cooperate.

I sensed the Lord was directing me and was willing to take the risk.

We drove with this man up alleys and across the city of over a million to a long, dark stairway, that headed up to a flat on the second floor. I was beginning to think I had made another bad decision. Dimitri wanted to wait in the car, but I eventually coaxed him with me up the stairs. A little old Ukrainian lady with a scarf on her head met us at the top and we entered.

I was introduced to a man who turned out to be the Billy Graham of the Ukraine. He had been ministering the Gospel for 50 years in his homeland.

President Reagan had called for the Berlin wall to come down, Gorbachev was in power and the Soviet Union was in collapse. Democracy was being embraced and free enterprise was on the rise. For the first time since the 1940's, this man had an opportunity to hold an open church service, above ground, and he was wasting no time.

He was putting together a crusade to be held only days from now. He had printed up posters, flyers and invitations and handed these out all over the city. He rented a huge civic center, complete with an orchestra pit, to hold this Gospel crusade. He called on the pastors of the underground church to have courage, come together, and preach the Gospel at this main event, which would be followed by a few other smaller events in different parts of the city.

What he said next would alter me forever.

He proceeded to tell me how a *window had opened* in the Ukraine to preach the Gospel and he didn't know for how long. We drank tea together and had a meal. He asked if I would play some music. I obliged and began to sing songs of worship as I felt led by the Holy Spirit's presence. I was in the presence of a real man of God, a saint who had witnessed terrible persecution and had an unwavering faith. This man was on a mission.

When I had finished one of the most intimate times of worship I have ever experienced, he said to me, "The church in my country has been under extreme persecution for decades. Churches have been burned, believers have been killed, and it has not been an easy road. But we are able to preach Jesus above ground now and I believe you are to be a part of these crusades."

Then he said those words I will never forget. He said, "Because you are from the West and wear 501 Levis, you have a platform to preach the Gospel. People will listen to you. I want you to preach the Gospel at our crusades."

I was speechless. These words were the *exact* words God had spoken to me, months earlier, through Dr. Josh McDowell at the Jesus Northwest festival in Washington state. I was experiencing a miracle right before my eyes. God had spoken to my heart and I had the hair-brained idea of driving my VW bus to Alaska and taking a ferry to Russia; now here I was, hearing this man of God utter the very words that got me moving to begin with.

I accepted the invitation. I had no idea what to expect, but neither did he. He had never done a crusade in the Ukraine before and didn't know if anybody would have the courage to show up.

The day arrived and they picked Dimitri and me up at the place we were staying. We showed up hours before it was to begin so we would have time to get everything set up. There were no fancy sound systems, no bells, and no whistles — just a mega phone, taped in the 'on' position and a stage.

People began to trickle in. I would peek out, periodically, from backstage and was amazed each time as more and more people would enter with looks of fear or apprehension on their faces.

We gathered with all the pastors in the back and prayed for revival, healing of the nation, repentance and salvation. When the time came to begin, the large man we had met in the park went out and, with a trembling voice, introduced the man I had met in the upstairs flat where he had invited me to come. Sasha was his name. He spoke a few words, prayed with everyone and then introduced me.

I took the stage in front of thousands of Christians and non-Christians alike who had seen more blood and suffering than any man should. They all had this fear in their eyes and were continuously looking around as if they were going to be arrested at any moment.

I introduced myself and, through interpretation, told them how God had spoken to me, months before, and asked me to come to the Ukraine. I told them I believed I had a message God wanted them to hear.

I would explain the songs and then sing them, since most of them could not understand English. I finished the first song and never had I experienced such a stoic crowd. Nothing. The song was over, but nothing. No acknowledgment of any kind. You could have heard a pin drop.

I began sweating bullets. I broke a guitar string on the next song, which I changed during the nauseating silence. I began the second song again and ended with a big finish, trying to loosen everybody up. There were a few folks who had the boldness to agree with the song and applaud, but it was a tough crowd.

Then, as I sang a few more songs, I felt the presence of God come down like I have rarely known. As I set my guitar down and began to share from the Word of God, a calm peace came over me. It was an experience I will never forget. I shared the passage from the Word about the Prodigal Son, and how the Father *ran* to the wayward son upon his return from rebellion. I focused on the loving father. God loved them, had not forgotten them and had a special place in His home for them.

I presented the Gospel in its simple, pure form and then sang another song and turned it back over to Sasha.

Sasha went back out and preached the Gospel with power, and the Holy Spirit did a work only He could do. As Sasha finished, everyone got up. Thousands of people just got up. It was weird. I asked Dmitri to tell me what was going on; he said Sasha had asked anyone who wanted to place his or her faith in Jesus to stand and come forward. Everyone did.

I realized that for many, this was the first time they had had an opportunity to publicly proclaim their faith. It was the first time many had heard the Gospel and been given an opportunity to respond. There were at least 5,000 people in the auditorium and it appeared as if all of them wanted to know Jesus and/or wanted to make a public profession of their faith.

It was so simple, so miraculous. It was the power of the Gospel.

My time in the Ukraine changed me forever because it taught me about the power of the Gospel. Never underestimate the power of the Gospel.

> *"I am not ashamed of the Gospel of Christ,*
> *it is the power of God unto salvation to those*
> *who will believe..."*
>
> *— The Apostle Paul*

Following this grand response to the Gospel, miracles took place as God initiated a time of healing. Many in the crowd began to cry out loudly how God had healed them in the moment. This was not a worked up "healing service". This was a genuine, God-inspired moment where he healed the sick and gave sight to the blind. Healing after healing took place, spontaneously, as the Holy Spirit fell upon that place.

I had never seen anything like it before, and I have never seen anything like it since.

Outside the auditorium that day, as I was talking with some Ukrainian students who were practicing their broken English, I noticed a little old lady weeping uncontrollably. It was not just an ordinary cry. It was the kind of weeping that comes up from the bottom of the soul, the kind of weeping that bursts out uncontrollably in moans of grief and sorrow. It reminded me of the way I cried in Jeff's VW that night back in Grants Pass — the night I placed my faith in Jesus for the first time, realized the destruction of my own sin and found freedom from it.

I noticed this little old woman — with her scarf wrapped over her head and around her little round face — but didn't recall the scene in my mind until days later. I asked Dimitri if he had noticed her. He told me he had spoken with her. She was weeping because she had not received one of the Bibles we gave out after the gathering. We only had a hundred or so Bibles and she was unable to fight her way to the front of the line to receive one. She was devastated.

This little Russian lady had traveled all the way from Siberia to visit family in Lvov and had heard about the crusade through a family member. She was part of a little church in Siberia that passed out hand-written copies of the Bible to read. The opportunity was so close for her to receive a complete copy of the Bible in her language, but she missed it. All the Bibles were given away and she was left without one.

"Tell me you found a Bible for her," I pressed Dimitri. He did, and said when he put that Bible in her hands, she clutched it to her chest like it was the most prized possession she would ever have. Indeed it was. Dimitri was certain she would die before releasing it to anyone as contraband.

Faith takes us on an unexpected journey. It might seem like it doesn't make sense at times and may even feel irresponsible. My trip to Ukraine certainly seemed like that. But our role isn't to judge the path where God leads us. Our role in this life is simply to obey the voice and the Spirit of God. In order to do that, I must abandon myself to the truth that God will work out the details.

I have to surrender to the knowledge that God will take me on a wild ride. I simply have to obey.

This is what faith looks like: giving when I don't have excess, leaving a job with every perk and benefit to make a home in a foreign land taking care of orphans, loving my neighbors and inviting them over for a BBQ while *knowing* many of them are gay, drug users and gang bangers. I can play it safe. I can live a normal, boring life filled with soccer games and TV. I can die, never having seen the miraculous power of God. Or, I can take risks, diving in headfirst, trusting God for the details. That's faith.

I have often thought of my trip to the Ukraine, the 501's, the crazy idea of driving my bus to Alaska and taking a Ferry to Siberia, the masses responding to the Gospel, the spontaneous outpouring of God's healing, and the little old lady weeping. These events have been branded into my soul. God took what seemed impossible and made it part of who I have become, in Him.

". . . With men this is impossible; but with God all things are possible."

— Jesus

If there are things God has placed in your heart and you feel they are too impractical or too impossible, think again. God is not looking for men or women with great ability to do His work. The only ability required is *avail*ability. Make yourself available to His service and your life will never be the same. Normal will become so bland that you won't believe you ever lived there. The adventure of trusting God and taking great risks will become a lifestyle you will never want to abandon. There are things God has for you that will shock you if you throw yourself upon His mercy.

His mercy is great and unlimited.

Before I left the Ukraine and began the long journey back home, I spent a few more days with the wonderful hostess who had opened up her home for Dimitri and me. Her name was Olga, a grandmother of six, and she had tirelessly tended to us both. She would rise in the predawn hours to go to the local markets and purchase food to cook us breakfast; then return in the afternoon to gather whatever was available. We ate a lot of soup made with cabbage and onions — somehow she was able to make everything more than palatable.

I really grew to love Olga while we were in the Ukraine and she didn't want us to leave. She treated us like kings and made sure we were always warm and well-fed. Though we spoke different languages, we begun to understand each other through body language, facial expressions and eye contact. We laughed a lot.

I tried to give her money as we departed but she would have none of it. She only accepted enough for the cost of the food at the marketplace and no more. I wanted so badly to give to her, but the only way it was going to happen was if I took the money and placed it under the top plate in her cupboard in the kitchen. The next time she set the table, the cash would be there for her.

As I pondered how much to give her, I felt like I should just give her the rest of what I had. It wasn't much, only a few hundred dollars, but for her, a few hundred dollars would feed her for a year. I already had all my train and plane tickets to get back, so I decided to give her all my money and keep only enough to buy some coffee and bagels on the trip home.

We said our goodbyes and Dimitri and I made our way to the train station.

We arrived in Warsaw in the evening, planning to find the dock for the train that would take us to Frankfurt, Germany the following afternoon before we went through customs. We had a long night ahead of us, but we were going to bundle up and try to get some sleep in the train station.

As we made our way through the Warsaw train station, we struggled to find anyone who spoke either English or Ukrainian. I was so exhausted and I just wanted to find the right dock so we could get some sleep. So I began roaming around, just obnoxiously yelling out in the corridors, "Anybody speak English? Anybody speak English?"

It was a man from Boston who heard my pleas and responded to me. He asked how he could help me and I told him I just needed to find the place where my next train would depart from the following day. I told him that, as soon as I found the corridor, I could get some rest. He was catching his train soon and didn't have a lot of time but brought his traveling companion with him to a ticket counter where they helped us out.

He asked where we had been and where we were from. I told him I had been in the Ukraine telling people about Jesus. He broke out in a big smile and as we talked for a few more minutes. He said, "Listen, I am an evangelist and am presently catching a train up north for the next several days. I want you and your friend to go to the hotel just a few blocks from here and use my room."

"It is fully paid for. All you need to do is go to the front desk and tell them you are Scott Campbell. Ask for the key to room number 205. They may or may not ask for ID. If they do, you're out of luck. But if they don't, use my room. It has two double beds. Feel free to use room service and get a good meal."

I was shocked and thanked him profusely as he walked away to board his train. I looked at Dimitri and said, "Lets give it a try."

We noted the dock where we were to catch our train the following day, grabbed our luggage and made our way to the hotel. As we walked, I prayed the front desk clerk at the hotel would just give us the key without any trouble. I was going to walk up to the desk like I owned the place and, with a confident voice, ask for my room key, number 205. We looked like we could easily have been traveling companions of the guy from Boston, so it just might work.

As we walked into the really nice hotel I began to get nervous. I told Dimitri to just act like we had been there before and to make his way to the elevators. I pranced up to the front desk, absolutely sure I was going to be arrested when they found out we were impostors, but kept my cool. I told them I was Scott Campbell and I wanted my key. They asked what room I was in and I told them, with somewhat of an angry voice, that I was in room 205 — and to hurry it up.

I held my bag and guitar and looked at them with eyes that said: *don't make me pull all my stuff out and dig for my ID*.

They bought it! They handed me the key and I grabbed it, turned and walked to the elevator where Dimitri stood, staring at me with eyes like a deer caught in the headlights.

We made our way to the room, dumped our gear on the floor and collapsed on the beds, laughing. We could not believe it. Hot showers, soft beds, room service — we were living! One moment we were trying to find a concrete floor where we could rest and then, minutes later, we were lying on soft beds, ordering room service.

I called my wife as we waited for the food we had ordered. It was the first time we actually had good connection for the past month. I told her of the momentous events of the past four weeks and how God had provided, again and again. Even as I spoke, I told her, food was on its way. This was an epic move of God's grace and more proof of his faithfulness. Food was on its way. *Food.*

We caught the train the next day and traveled through Germany. From there, we got on our plane to Portland, where I had parked my old VW bus. My wife surprised me by showing up in Portland to greet me when I got off of the plane. I was so ecstatic to see her — we talked late into the night as I told her, firsthand, the power of God I had experienced.

By now, I was completely ruined for anything but living by faith. No adventure compared to this. There was nothing even close to leaping out in faith as the Lord spoke; nothing like trusting Him for the details. God was faithful to work through anyone who would be obedient to the prompting of His Holy Spirit. God could use anyone to share His Gospel. All I had to do was make myself available and be obedient. He would take care of the rest, right down to the very detail, even providing a bed to sleep on — and *room service* — in a freak encounter with a stranger from Boston who happened to be catching a train in Warsaw.

These kinds of details were mind boggling to me; but with God, nothing is impossible.

I was learning a life of obedience to the prompting of the Holy Spirit and the Word of God was unparalleled to any other way of life. Normal was routine and predictable. Faith in God, on the other hand, was exciting and adventurous. Faith was believing God for the impossible and putting myself in positions where, if God didn't come through, all was lost.

But all is never lost. It was the great, young missionary Jim Elliot who said, "He is no fool who gives what he cannot keep to gain that which he cannot lose." We have nothing to lose and everything to gain as we live a life abandoned to our great and merciful Father.

EPILOGUE

I have a Father now. God has adopted me as His own. I will never be abandoned, rejected or disowned. I am loved by my Father. He will never beat me or tear me down. I never fear abuse and understand the discipline of my heavenly Father is always for my good.

My Father really cares and is constantly looking out for my best interests. Because of Him, I am a man of hope. I know my future holds great things because my Father holds my future and desires great things for me. He is a great Father and always will be.

The chain of sin has been broken in my life — addiction, hatred, bitterness and anger no longer control me. The power of sin has been broken and I am no longer a slave to it. The same can be true for you.

> *"Sin is no longer your master, for you no longer live under the requirements of the law. Instead, you live under the freedom of God's grace."*

> *— The Apostle Paul*

Because I am free, I absolutely love living life. The journey is a great adventure as I live each day by faith and expectation. God is at work and has prepared good things for me to walk in. Now I live each day just going about my Father's business, bringing Him glory and showing the world around me how He is good.

Our past certainly shapes us but it does not have to define us.

I still have my quirks and still deal with issues related to my past — but who doesn't? The staggering difference is I am not defined by my past. My identity is not in what happened to me as a child or the traumatic events of my history. My identity is completely wrapped up in Jesus Christ. I am a slave by choice, completely submitted to Him as my Lord and King.

I am free of bitterness and hatred. I am no longer trying to "find myself".

Some would say I am in denial, that I will always be an addict, and it is impossible to be totally healed. All I can say is that I was blind, and now I can see.

God is still in the business of healing and restoration today. He is just as much a miracle-worker as He was when He spoke the worlds into existence and raised the dead. He is the same God, unchanged forever.

There is not a wound He cannot heal.

There is not a past He cannot redeem.

There is not a tear He cannot wipe away.

Not a sickness He cannot heal.

Not an addiction He cannot break.

Not a relationship He cannot restore.

Not a man or woman He cannot change.

Not a sinner He cannot save.

My clarity.

My stability.

My anchor in an angry sea.

My Rock.

My Compass in a raging tide.

I live and breathe by His amazing grace,

Unearned and undeserved.

"God showed His great love for us by sending Christ to die for us while we were still sinners."

— The Apostle Paul

I found my true north.

He was with me all along!

As this book was going to print, I received this letter from my son and it made me realize: The

Character of our earthly father does not have to determine the mothers or fathers we will be.

Read carefully:

Mountains and Run Down Houses

My dad makes me think of two things: mountains and run down houses. We all have different aspects of our personality, a thousand bits and pieces that form to make us who we are. But generally there are only two or three that truly define us, character traits we are born with that either grow or shrink based upon how we live. Mountains and run down houses are the two elements I believe make my dad, Jim Wright, who he is.

From the beginning of time mountains have been a metaphor for higher living.

Closer to God.

Closer to the sun.

Distant from the wars and chaos below.

Peaceful, clear.

So many critical moments in the Bible took place on a mountain top. Why somewhere far removed from the cities, the hustle and bustle of daily life? Because in order to reach the heights, the mountain must be climbed. And the tallest mountains always yield the most beautiful view, the clearest air. There is no easy way to get to the top. You have to prepare, train, build your endurance, pack the right equipment, and once all those things have been done, you begin to climb.

One foot in front of the other.

Through the day.

Through the night.

Fall asleep on a bed of snow.

Wake up, put one foot in front of the other, again.

It's one thing to climb a mountain out of necessity, but it's something else entirely to do so when the immovable piece of earth is not in your way. It's something different when you feel the need to climb it simply because it's there. And it's beautiful. And it's hard.

This is one of the most important lessons my dad taught me while growing up − that we should never be afraid to take on something because it will be hard to accomplish.

One foot in front of the other.

This applies to work, family, art, and life.

Most often the hardest things in life that we undertake turn out to be the most rewarding.

This is as true for mountains as it is for relationships.

My dad started out climbing rocks — big jutting pieces that stuck up out of the ground and could be scaled in ten to fifteen minutes. Gradually he looked for bigger rocks, harder climbs. It's no surprise he eventually moved on to climbing ice-covered peaks that took multiple days to complete.

I want to say something cliché about this, but I won't.

The fact is, something is hard when you don't know how to do it. If you take the time to learn, are willing to fail and willing to fall, it won't take long before climbing a boulder feels easy and you'll be looking for something taller.

It reminds me of what President Kennedy said about sending a man to the moon.

"We don't do these things because they are easy, but because they are hard."

My dad taught me that.

I don't think work ethic can be taught; I think you either have it or you don't. But if you do have it, the importance of putting it to use can be taught. I think I've always had a willingness to work at things, whether it be a job or learning to play the guitar. But my dad taught me how vital this trait was to being a solid man in a shaky world.

The thing about my dad is, he can't not fix things. And I don't mean he tinkers with engines in the garage. I mean he sees something big, like a house, and envisions what it could be with a whole lot of elbow grease.

Growing up we lived on several different mission bases in Mexico and Honduras. Each one of those places was left with Jim Wright's mark on it. He built, he reinforced, he created. He put his skills as a carpenter to use and left each base stronger and more intact than when we arrived.

Every house we lived in has his additions, remodels, and repairs all over it.

It's no wonder that in the School of Ministry, he taught young men how to use their hands to build something lasting.

If you drive to Camp Bradley you'll see rows of small cabins that were designed and constructed by my dad and his rag-tag crew. If you drive to our old house on Palm Street you'll see a backyard that didn't exist before we moved in. You'll see a fence that wasn't there. If you drive to my grandma's house you'll see another fence and countless other small signs that my dad has been there. If you drive to where he and my mom live now, you'll see a completely different house than the one they purchased.

On and on it goes.

I think this trait of repairing physical structures wherever he goes is also true of the people he meets along the way.

Repairing spiritual structures. Rebuilding human beings.

What he taught me was this; whatever you put your hand to, do it the best you can.

Notice these two elements of mountains and run down houses are very much rooted in the physical world. This may seem an odd connection for me to make regarding a man who is currently the pastor of his own church. This is because Jim Wright was a father before he was a pastor. He is not my pastor; he is my dad. He is very much a man in the physical world and he has always understood that a man must work to provide for his family. He must work to have purpose and be fulfilled.

Don't be afraid to do something because it's hard.

Whatever you do, do it well.

These two lessons just about sum up manhood. They sum up what it takes to be a provider, a husband, a father, a friend.

Within this structure, much can be built, but without these two things there is very little protection from the world.

Throughout my childhood my dad tried to teach me a lot of things. Some more successfully than others. I'm still no good at working on cars and I'm a pretty terrible *carpenter. I don't usually know how things work and I get frustrated whenever I have to mow the lawn or pick weeds. But, I have never been afraid to pop the hood of my Isuzu Rodeo and start banging away at it. I've never been afraid to try and figure out why something isn't working. Whether I get to the bottom of the problem isn't the point. I don't live in fear. And the things I do know how to do, I do with absolutely everything I have.*

This applies to my job, my marriage, my children, and my art.

I am incredibly grateful that these lessons were taught to me at an early age, by someone who loved me. I didn't have to learn them after being fired from my job and losing my house.

Now that I'm a father myself, I often think about the lessons I want to teach my boys the lessons that will help them become great men. And I always come back to these two lessons my father taught me a long time ago. Lessons that don't fade but only get brighter with age.

Someone once said your legacy is your children. If that's true, then I consider mountains and run down houses to be the legacy I pass down to my boys. My two men-in-training.

Thank you dad for teaching me what it means to be strong.

Thank you for teaching me the value and importance of hard work.

Thank you for showing me every task, no matter how small, is important and should be undertaken with full intention to see it through to the end.

If the body is the temple in which the spirit dwells, I believe these lessons are the doors and walls, the floors and ceiling of a house where faith can live.

Thank you.

Happy 50th Birthday.

Love, Your son